Burning

A JOURNAL

BY THE SAME AUTHOR

THE BLUE MOUNTAINS TRILOGY
The Waterlily
Dear You
The Mountain

ANTHOLOGY (CO-EDITED)
The Penguin Book of Australian Women Poets

POETRY
Trader Kate and the Elephants
Luxury
Honey
Figs
Selected Poems
Crosshatched

ESSAYS
The Floral Mother

TRAVEL
Angels and Dark Madonnas
(India and Italy)
Lilies, Feathers and Frangipanni
(New Zealand and the Cook Islands)
Gorillas, Tea and Coffee
(Africa)

Burning

A JOURNAL

KATE LLEWELLYN

HUDSON
HAWTHORN

Published by Hudson Publishing

PO Box 537 Hawthorn, Victoria 3122
Copyright © Kate Llewellyn, 1997

First published 1997

Set in 10.5/14pt Garamond by the publishers

Printed in Australia by
Southwood Press, Marrickville, New South Wales

Cover design based on the painting, *Conversations with Sicillia*,
by Pat Harry

National Library of Australia cataloguing in publication data:

Llewellyn, Kate.
Burning: a journal.

ISBN 0 949873 63 2

1. Llewellyn, Kate – Diaries.
2. Women poets, Australian – 20th century – Diaries.
I. Title.

A 821.3

To Pat Harry, with gratitude

October

2nd October, Monday. South Ballina Caravan Park.
Whip birds woke me. Over and over, the whip sound flicked the mind. No wind on the banksias and gums after last night's storm. They hang like a painting outside the caravan's window. The banksia's brown furred fruits sit as if they are stuffed animals poking out among the dark green leaves.

I took down the curtains to see better and made tea. Nobody is about.

A clear blue sky and birds. Lying in bed looking at the sky, last night's dreams lying like leaves waiting to be raked, I decided to start a book in the form of a diary.

I have come here because it is a long weekend, unable to face the days alone in a flat in Lismore where I know nobody. Working at the University there for the past eight weeks has been a pleasure. I've been going to Peri's farm for weekends but it is occupied now for the school holidays. So, after giving a talk at Ballina, it seemed a good idea to stay on for a few days. I can't afford a motel and besides many of them are depressing. A chill enters me as I walk in.

Betty (one of the women at the talk) gave me a lift here. We arrived three days ago with fish from a shop on the way, and a basket of red hippeastrum lilies, red geraniums and white daisies given to me for the talk. There is also a bag of books. Vegetables in a box from Tina, the market gardener near the University.

Betty, seeing the bare mattress in this caravan, set off and returned with sheets and a doona. I hadn't known that linen isn't provided in rented caravans. She also brought matches for the gas stove.

The grey raked sand around the caravan is like a Japanese garden. White flannel flowers bloom under the low trees. Wattle birds and sparrows are calling. I am happy.

My friends Rosie and Jack are separating. While lightning shot gold cracks across the grey sky, I sat at the blue public phone and talked to Rosie. She is leaving Jack after eighteen years. People were coming in and out of the shop buying milk and papers, banging the wire screen door, as we talked.

I went back to my caravan shaken. These are two of my oldest friends. We've travelled together and been through everything. He helped me through my divorce and I helped him through his. Rosie's been an incomparable friend, nursed me when I was sick. She's given a dozen parties for us as Jack and my birthdays coincide.

Later the storm cracked open and rain poured down. It began to come in through the raised air vent of my caravan. I wrenched it shut with an effort and got into bed. It was five o'clock. After two hours silence fell. Then fireworks began to erupt in the town across the bay. Golden chrysanthemums exploded while people called and clapped and children cried out with pleasure. It is the Queen's Birthday holiday.

This is a good place to read Patrick White. It is so Australian here – the sound of surf, the white flannel flowers, people in bathers strolling to the bathrooms in thongs with a towel over the shoulder. On arrival I read some of his stories and now *Voss*, a masterpiece. Voss has just set off inland. I went to the world premiere of the opera at the Adelaide Festival. Marilyn Richardson was Laura Trevelyan in a blue taffeta dress.

There is an empty beach 22 kilometres long only a short sandy track away. This is nearly the most eastern part of Australia. (Byron

Bay is the furthest east.) Long breakers roll in and burst on the sand like sighs of the universe. For miles a frill of round pink jelly fish lie dying on the sand. They are interspersed every few metres with bright blue stingers like embroidered forget-me-nots, with a long thread the embroiderer hasn't cut off trailing among the pink roses of jelly fish stitched for miles on the sand. The hem of the sea.

Walking for an hour I saw nobody. Only a small low fishing boat out at sea. Then a motorcyclist appeared from nowhere. I tugged my hat further down and strode towards the cyclist looking ferocious. While I was walking on a road in the rainforest last week at Mount Glorious, a motorcyclist, after making an obscene gesture, turned round and followed me. Suddenly I realised we were alone. Tranquillity evaporated. Fear arrived. This one on the beach though was harmless and rode by.

Spray joins the sky and sea in an aura of pale air until everything is invisible except the sand underfoot and the nearest wave, crashing, spilling out and receding, like a withdrawn offer.

People outside the caravan are stirring. "You leaving are you?" "Yeah." Lying here as if in a hammock of banksias, birds calling, the white stars of fallen flannel flowers on the grey sand, I can smell chops.

Later

Pelicans stand on the shore watching a man and a boy casting into the surf. From time to time one rises up flapping slowly over the big waves, cruising on a draught of air, moving its wings indolently. Their surprising feet are like blue leather gloves. They make tracks on the sand, their toes pointing into their waddle. A man sits on the shore putting on flippers and then strides into the surf with just the same waddle.

Today, after nobody and nothing yesterday, surfers have appeared. They stand, capital letters on the sentences of the waves. Others sit on the dunes in black wet suits watching. Tan sea eagles with black heads and tail tips stand on every hillock. They might be Masai standing on a hill looking out over the plain at zebra. All the birds need are red blankets and sticks. The clouds lie in the mirror of the wet sand. A flock of brown birds sweeps over the sea.

When I returned after three hours, the old woman in the unit next door called out. She asked what I was doing here. Her daughter is a joint owner of the park.

"My name is Ivy Moss. That's my wedding photograph," she said as invited I stepped inside her home.

"It was 1930. I was 21."

"What was your husband's name?"

"Moss."

"I mean what else?"

"Fred Moss. We were married 58 years."

"You must have taken good care of him."

We chatted on while Ivy showed me how to cover coathangers in foil and knitted nylon fabric. She gave me one from a pile she'd been making. There was a framed copy of a 1967 advertisement for her dressmaking school on the wall.

Later she called "Kate! Here's a sample of the nylon you'll need for the coat-hangers. You might forget when you go to the shop." The sample was pinned to a paper on which instructions were carefully written in ink.

"I'm 87" she said, hiding half her face with her hand held against one side of her nose, confiding as if on stage.

The wind has come flapping and scratching the trees against the black and white striped canvas entrance to this caravan. Apart from the stability of the wicker couch I am lying on, this could be sailing.

Four nights ago, when I arrived, I thought 'Now I know where criminals hide'. But now that thought seems ridiculous and it feels just as safe as anywhere else.

Until last month it had been a year since I had written any poems. I came here to begin again. It was for a commission for the *Floriade* Festival in Canberra from Peter Haines the curator of the

Lanyon Gallery. He invited me to write a suite of poems to accompany the wildflower painting show by Beryl Martin. Then Professor Leon Cantrell here suggested they be set to music and introduced Michael Hannan the composer to me. Michael said he'd like to set the poems into a song cycle for Ghillian Sullivan to sing.

Michael, sitting beside me in my office in the University at Lismore last month, said he believes it is important to keep working at composing, or the ability vanishes. And so it has proved to be for me with poetry. The wheels creaked. Then suddenly thirteen poems in a few weeks. It doesn't mean of course that they will all be included, but it's a start.

Pig Face
(Disphyma clavellatum)

Nothing except tamarisk,
daisy bushes and I grow here
beside the enchanted bay.

I stare at the sun.
Although there's seldom rain
my leaves are grey tubes of sap.

Despised plant
with a name from derision,
I am not to blame.
A survivor,
the guilt is not mine.
Violet, lily and hyacinth,
the flower shop belles,
cannot grow here in the spray.

I am salt's bride
brought home to rocks, sand and sun.

Change my name.

Michael said he's fond of a song cycle by Ravel that uses cello, flute and piano and that he will probably write for these instruments.

5th October, Thursday. Lismore.

Alison and I had lunch. She is the University librarian and over the past nine weeks we've become friends. Restrained, elegant, forty, she raises hands to the world as if she's being held up at gun point whenever she's telling a story. I told her about Rosie and Jack separating. Then, while we were talking, I suddenly saw the situation in the way others might: that Jack and I have been such good friends over twenty years that we might now have an affair. But we're not going to make that mistake.

Together, Alison and I started a campaign to buy 200 titles of Australian women writers' fiction for the shelves. The fundraising party we held didn't make money, but from talking about it, things started to happen. Money came from somewhere, and the books were bought.

It reminded me of Group Captain Cheshire, who said that when he began to build houses for the sick in India that it was only necessary to begin. He took a wheelbarrow and wheeled a load of bricks to the site. He had no money. It was just the act of that first load that led to people helping him. Now there are buildings.

Years ago, when I was pregnant, our Italian neighbour, Mr Catalano, had a big grapevine he didn't want because he was extending his house over it. I knew I couldn't carry it. But I started to dig a small trench for it near our back door. Great Uncle Stan, deaf and halt from the First World War, came to visit. He was over 80. When he saw me digging he took the spade and finished the digging. Then we went to get the vine with the wheelbarrow. Together, the woman six months pregnant and the old man got the vine across the road. My husband, in his wheelchair, asked me to turn him around because he couldn't bear to watch.

Mr Catalano told us to lay the main trunk down as a root in the trench and lash the branches to a post. We did, and within two years the vine covered the trellis. From then on we ate under it in summer and the grapes hung down like bunches of sweet tears. Mrs Catalano used to sit under her own vine with a board on her knees rolling gnocchi with her thumb. I didn't have the sense to ask her for the recipe.

8th October, Sunday. Leura.

After four months, home. Last night I stayed in Sydney with Hugh my son and his wife Cathy. Because Cathy had a meeting in the mountains she drove me here, with luggage. As we drove down the Mall, the cherry blossom was almost finished. Leaves have sprouted all over the trees, although the Leura Fair is tomorrow and pink cherry blossom always fills the streets then. Forget-me-nots have made their blue swathe through my garden.

My daughter Lily is packing to go to New York and Rome tomorrow. We rolled up black clothes into a black bag. Sam, her six-year-old son, is to stay with me and go to school.

This is my new role. The centre of the stage is no longer mine. I feel as if I am dancing on one side of it, not unhappy, intrigued in a way. While not exactly relieved, I am at least resolved that this is how it is going to be from now on, and how it ought to be. It is not uncomfortable – just new. I think it may save a lot of strain and effort. While not exactly a sock-mender, I am now part of a back-up team.

My neighbours Nan and Phil invited us over for champagne at eleven this morning, to say goodbye to Lily. We sat under an umbrella with the garden roaring around us, the green like a bite, azaleas pink as a yawn. Phil is to have a heart operation shortly and this gives more meaning to such things.

In my living room Lily's computer is on a table draped with a white sheet like an altar. Before this year is out I plan to master it. My own machine is on the dining room table. On it is Rosie's desert painting with its quotation from Baudelaire, a relic of the desert trip of 5,000 kilometres in two weeks we did this winter. That trip calmed me, cleared my mind. Being in a desert is rather like being high up in a plane over a continent. A perspective on trouble is reached. Though difficulties do not exactly fade away, they certainly recede. Now I am hoping to hang on to this calmer feeling. It was partly the lack of ceilings that helped. Stars, silence, sand dunes and wildflowers, camp fires at night, turquoise and pink dawns, and a gold moon burning relentlessly.

9th October, Monday. Leura.

School begins again today. I packed Sam's lunch in the way I had been shown by Lily. Friends took him because he hasn't yet got a bus pass.

It is cold and silver. After four months, first in the desert and then at Lismore, the cold feels keen.

After school Sam and I went to the oval with a football. I taught him the difference between an overall and an oval, and an addict and an attic.

"You're nicer since you've been away," he remarked.

"Is that so? Why?"

"You'll let me watch television until I fall asleep."

The reason I have agreed to this is so he won't miss his mother as he did last night. I'd said "Let's pray for Mum and Dad." He said a prayer for his father. Then I said "Aren't you going to ask God to take care of Mum?" He said "No, I'm going to do that." I said "I see" and he added "I'll ask God to make me brave."

10th October, Tuesday. Leura.

A plane is due to take off right now for New York with Lily on board. Naturally I am worried. But the anxiety of parents is amusing to children until they become parents. Even then they are still likely to find it so, unless it is a case of their own child. I suppose people need to live with daring and feel immortal.

This place smells. I put eighty kilos of Dynamic Lifter and twenty of blood-and-bone on the garden. Kill or cure. After almost a decade azaleas are like white flags under the trees. And it was fertiliser and water that did it. Nan and I drove to the nursery and bought tomatoes, basil, petunias, capsicum and pink impatiens.

When I first came I thought it was called patience and I planted a lot which died from frost. I did not know that it is a spring plant here. This garden is a pleasure. There are times when it's tended and others when it's left. Dogwood, planted when I came, are tall and blooming now. Strawberry-pink and cream foxgloves are about to bloom.

Yesterday, as I was mopping the floor, I picked up a card, the nine of spades. Carmen Jones sings "Da nine!" She knows she's going to die. It did not occur to me for a moment that it could mean I'm about to but I thought it might mean somebody I love is.

11th October, Wednesday. Leura.
Bright rags of clouds were drifting high up in the blue when I drew the curtains this morning. Burgundy prunus leaves and the pale green of the climbing rose waved against the window. Sam and I lay there watching. Then we played noughts and crosses on the ceiling. The white ceiling is crossed with brown slats of wood, and these make six squares. By adding three below in our minds it is possible to play noughts and crosses staring up. I hope it teaches him to see things that aren't there. This is not exactly exhilarating for me, but it has a pleasurable tender quality.

Two metres of Mudgee ironbark wood were delivered onto the footpath yesterday. After throwing 100 kilos of fertiliser around I left the wood sitting there.

Sam caught the wrong bus from school. He arrived home hot, red-faced and late. I was standing in the drive worrying.

"I got the Wentworth Falls bus. I had to walk from the train station."

He'd had to cross several roads to get home and he's never been allowed to cross even one before.

"A woman helped me across a road and I waved to her."

Yesterday was the first time he's been alone on a bus as his mother drives. He'd said then "I'm nervous" and I'd asked if he'd like me to go on the bus with him but he'd said no. When the bus came, he got in and waved.

There are dried bananas here on the sink. They came from an Italian Australian called Tindara who has a shop in her garage in Lismore. For days, walking past on the way to work, I saw a board with a list of the fruit and vegetables for sale. Down the sloping cement drive, written in chalk, was a sign 'Down there to Tina's shop.' One day, needing an avocado for lunch, I walked down by the side of a two-storey brown brick house. It seemed deserted, doors open but nobody about. I called out.

Further down the hillside I could see bananas growing, lettuce, onion beds and Italian salad greens. Tina, in black gum boots, was climbing laboriously up towards me. She took me into her shop with its roll-up door in the side of the house. There she had a great deal of fruit and vegetables, much bricolage; peach jam, eggplant in oil, dried bananas, tomato chutney, and so on.

Two of Tina's granddaughters were there for the school holidays. Lithe and brown-haired, Virginia and Louise, they stood beside their grandmother who was like an ancient olive tree with two young saplings on either side. They love the shop. It is like a playhouse to them. I asked if they too would be market gardeners one day. "No," Tindara said. "They go to university, get good jobs. This too hard work. Too much work."

I explained that I had not known from the board at the gate that the produce was homegrown, and said that she would sell more if the sign said it was organically grown. Tina said that she had trouble writing in English, so I made a notice which we stuck next to hers.

From then on I called in almost daily. "You have, you have," Tina would say pushing extra ladyfinger bananas or mandarins into my bag. I'd get to work with a bag stuffed with leaves and jars of antipasto.

I asked what Tina was short for. "Tindara. I Tindara. You know. She Black Madonna." She went into another room and came back with a newsletter from the Vatican (to which she subscribes) with a picture of a carved black Madonna on the cover. She is Sicilian and this is a North African Madonna.

Then I was told a story about the Black Madonna. A miracle had occurred when somebody put their sick child into the arms of the Madonna statue. They looked away and suddenly the child was gone. "Where you put my baby?" Then the parent looked out of the window and saw that the sea had parted, and on the sand, surrounded by sea, the child sat playing.

I stood there, wishing I had a tape-recorder.

Another morning Tindara was cutting ladyfinger bananas in halves and putting them on a wire tray to dry. I asked if that was all that was needed. "Fan-force oven," she said. Then she ran next door and brought out fruit from a downstairs room. This house she told me is also hers. She sold her farm but kept enough land for the market garden. An old white Queenslander house on stilts was once in this garden. The University had bought it and used it for a time as a residence for visiting staff.

So here is another story of a migrant who, simply by keeping her culture, has been immensely successful and happy. This gardener, even after thirty years or so away, could stand in a Sicilian plot and look as though she had never left her country.

I can't do the washing-up because the outlet is blocked. Tree roots block the drain pipes here about once a year and the plumber is coming. It's a bore waiting for him.

I am wondering if skylights in these rooms would not only light but heat them. If clear glass could be used the sun could come in and at night the stars could be seen. In New Zealand at Huka Lodge the bathrooms have clear glass ceilings. From the bath you can watch pine needles floating. That was one of the most memorable things about that place, and there were many others. A man is coming to measure and quote for skylights today, along with the plumber I hope.

Anchored here, I tip out drawers. The contents of drawers make me wonder. Why did I keep a bundle of scraps of material from my wedding dress? Did I think I'd have it altered and use it again? Or wear it so often it would need repairs?

Once, after a very busy weekend, my friend Rosie walked into her bedroom, flung open her wardrobe doors and began to tip out wire drawers to tidy them. This impressed me. As soon as I got home I did the same to a chest-of-drawers. Ever since it has been kept tidy. This does not run in the family so it's been an effort as well as a pleasure. People who go to boarding school are probably taught to be tidy. I wonder if it is really a learnt thing or simply genetic. After an incredible five generations of military men, Sam's paternal grandfather is so tidy that, to this day, he simply whisks the top shirt from an immaculate pile and dons it.

Judgements made on tidiness go far beyond the rational. An untidy woman is felt to have an element of sluttishness in her. That is why I kick things under the bed when certain visitors are coming. It is fear. Yet extreme tidiness can be depressing. Entering a very tidy, austere house, I'm overtaken by feelings of both depression and claustrophobia. But then a very untidy house has just the same effect.

Nothing in a woman's life, except children, matches the power housework has to induce guilt. When did it begin? The woman in a cave may have arranged the bones outside her entrance tidily, and stacked the fallen rocks in a neat pile because it was safer. Possibly the woman in the cave next door boasted of her own superior industry. Or her mate did. It is tied up with hygiene and is related to competition. Whatever else is involved it is in our culture and one of the most powerful forces keeping women controlled, submissive – and at times frenzied. Yet the woman who stays at home to work at keeping her home clean and tidy, is also at times derided.

There is nothing I have read in feminist writing that sanctifies the woman who works away from home. Yet millions feel guilty and inadequate because they make a home for themselves and others and don't bring in an extra income. What kind of a society values earning money over home-making?

As a feminist I have always been among those who consider any man's underestimation of child-rearing and housework blind and mistaken. But now, without the current being seen to change, somehow it has and some women talk today just as some men did in the Seventies, and before.

12th October, Thursday. Leura.

Red and green parrots flew out from the beech trees over the footpath as we opened the gate this morning. It is almost hot. Two skylights are to go in today. I have a million things to do but have been doing housework instead of meeting deadlines. Possibly the fault of my outburst yesterday. Also, for the first time in a decade, I have somebody coming to clean this afternoon.

Now that the plumber has been taps can run again. If one ever feels superior it is only necessary to watch a plumber at work on your drains to put things in perspective. Tree roots make his visit at least annual. It is possible to spend a lot more and get pipes that are root-proof, but I'd rather not.

The verandah is about to fall down. It needs new flooring. And people often tell me to buy a dishwasher and a clothes drier.

While living in a frugal way most of the time, I suddenly lash out and buy something extravagant. My friend Jane once said, after we'd bought shoes, "By God, when you get the bit between your teeth you really go." One of the things I found most difficult about marriage (while liking many things about it) was the spending of money. It is a tremendous relief not to have a husband when returning from shopping.

For half an hour I waited on the path for the school bus. Yesterday, as Sam had missed the bus to Leura, the headmistress drove him home. Today he tells me he is late because the driver stopped and went to talk to his girlfriend while the children were allowed out to play on the path. I said "What!" Not sure what to do about this, I am thinking.

13th October, Friday. Leura.

Light pours down. Skylights illuminate the room in a way that has me looking up wondering why the light switch has been left on. It gives the room a curiously uplifting effect.

I am looking up Herodotus because I think he may be the world's first travel writer and today I have a travel book to review. The *Oxford Classical Dictionary* says:

> His style probably owes little to the early logographers, whose scanty fragments hardly reveal any style at all... To Homer he undoubtedly owes much, in cast of thought as well as in language... What other literary influences may have gone to the moulding of him is hard to say. Nor is it easy to analyse the surpassing beauty of his prose, for Herodotus has *no mannerisms* [my emphasis]... hardly a single technical device can be said to be characteristic of Herodotus. Each is used when and only when it is needed...

"Music is speech without words," a conductor has just told Margaret Throsby on radio. Now Act II of *Fidelio* is playing; green and sublime.

16th October, Monday. Leura.

It's quiet. Sam's at school. Our friends have gone home. I have been watering the strawberries the children planted in tubs yesterday.

John's group of psychiatrists had a conference at the Little Company Guest House over the weekend. John's wife Ghilly and their two daughters came along too. On Saturday morning she brought Stephanie and Donna over and, talking over the heads of the children, we walked to the park. We discussed our friends Rosie and Jack separating. The ripples from their tragedy affect us all. At lunch at Bon-Ton we sat near the fountain while the children threw gravel in it and Sam tried to fish out coins.

That night we went to dinner at the guest house where I gave a talk by the fire. When we arrived John was sitting at the piano and he took the sheet of music William Evans had sent me, the setting of a song he'd composed called *Lilies*, from a poem of mine.

Lilies

*In the green green heart of the forest
arum lilies bloom*

pools of pure white light

*arriving at the lilies every night
the lovers pause and join
then continue through the forest*

*all night at every pool of lilies
they join again
together
(the light fell on a breast
and it became a lily)
the forest shelters them
with the covering of night
(her breast felt smooth as lilies)*

*and at dawn the lovers come out
to see the pale pink sky
above a field of grass
so they greet the day together*

*every night
they enter the forest*

William Evans is only seventeen. I met him at a book launch at Lilianfels resort last year. He said then he'd send me some of his work.

A child in a long white dress and brown hair walked in with her father Geoff. John played and we all stood and listened.

Yesterday John and Ghilly came here and brought with them Geoff and his wife Pauline. Geoff is a psychiatrist now but he was once Edna Walling's GP. He said, after a look at the garden, it reminded him of Edna's. I told him it had been made attempting to follow her ideas. He remarked that the house is like hers too, but lighter. If I had paid more attention to the house and garden, been a little more energetic, I would not have been so surprised. As a beginner, when I came here, I tried to make a garden using Edna's principles but without understanding. A form of passionate ignorance can lead to learning. Before I read the Walling books bulbs were planted in rows.

At lunchtime we had a barbecue down at the swings on the edge of the escarpment, with the blue valley below stretching away to infinity.

Pauline, a social worker, has multiple sclerosis. I don't think I have seen MS in the early stages before. Passing sausages to me, she asked "Would you like a cat?" We laughed lightly, but Geoff, returning from cooking, said tenderly "There may be something more sinister behind it."

I was reminded of what Dr Johnson said about memory loss. If a young man leaves his hat in a restaurant and returns to fetch it, his friends at the table do not remark on it except to say that he forgot his hat. If an old man does this, they say that he is losing his memory.

Because my husband had had polio and was in a wheelchair, I see children with handicapped parents in a way I didn't at the time see my own. I know now some of the effects, the difficulties, grief and shame they can feel. I know how hard it is for them to come to terms with all this years later. Each situation, though similar, is very different and Geoff's and Pauline's daughters may be helped more than I managed to help my own children. My attitude was "Well, we are lucky to have him. He's been close to death so we should rejoice. Any of him is better than nothing." And so I tried to treat everything as normal. I expected my children to understand this although I never explained it to them. This was a mistake. Then when the divorce came things went awry even more.

Later

Nan drove me to Katoomba to shop. The sun poured onto the asphalt outside K-Mart. People were going about their lives, shopping with the dog.

I have been buying four cartons of custard at a time for Sam. On the way home Nan told me her recipe for French custard and now there is one in the oven. It's simple and good. This is the way it's made:

> Separate 4 eggs.
>
> Beat the yolks with 1 cup sugar, 1/2 cup sherry, 1 tsp vanilla and 1 tbsp plain flour.
>
> Heat 1 litre of milk and pour this onto the yolk mixture.
>
> Gently fold in the whipped egg whites and bake 1 1/2 hours in a moderate oven with the dish sitting in a pan of hot water.

Here is Nan appearing as a character in a book. But to me she is this neighbour, this gardener, this wife of almost fifty years, this grandmother, giving a recipe, shopping with a friend. The smiling dignity and wisdom with which she walks with me round her garden is one of the pleasures of my life. Her husband Phil comes out in shorts and gum boots and joins us at the brown table under a tree. We gossip, laugh and part. Once, a year or two ago, we walked together down the garden and suddenly one of those moments happened when I thought 'This is wonderful. We may never be like this again, everything exuberant in the sun, our affection and tenderness and amusement, all here together.' It was like this today too. I wrote a poem about it.

How can a book capture a character when the pleasure she gives is so private, so individual? For that matter, when and why do we, as readers, find the ordinary extraordinary? What are we seeking when we read? I have been looking at an old *Anteus* magazine full of writers on reading. William Gass is quoted:

> We are so pathetically for this other life, for the sounds of distant cities and the sea; we long to pit ourselves against some trying wind, to follow the fortunes of a ship hard beset, to face up to

murder and fornication, and the sombre results of anger and love; oh, yes, to face up – in books.

And the great American poet Donald Hall writes:

> Literature is largely, although not entirely, the product of maniacs... Any notion that connects genius with abnormal psychology is routinely dismissed with the epithet romantic. Conventional minds need to dismiss the notion of functional aberration. But discovery necessitates eccentricity because the centre is already known. Of course it must be noted the neither mania nor anything else guarantees discovery.

Someone once said "Some people say life's the thing. I prefer books." A reader, a children's nurse, wrote to me last week: "I found a line in a Carol Shield's short story recently that describes me. I thought you'd understand it. 'She was the kind of woman who reads everything... print is her way of entering and escaping the world'."

It is not just a matter of getting vicarious thrills from reading. We live like blind moles but occasionally the curtain of blindness is rent. We suddenly see something about life and its mysteries and often it is in reading that we do this.

'Jesu joy of man's desiring' is playing on the radio. The custard's cooked. No it's not. The stove's gone out. I need a new one.

Increasingly I am interested in attempting what my friend Peri tells me she has decided to do. This is to abandon rancour. I thought 'Trust you to decide that'.

Yesterday she rang to say goodbye before flying to India with her daughter Sheridan for three weeks. I said "I must love you very much as I am only a little bit jealous. Just for the pleasure of hearing the names, tell me where you are going." So she began, "Hyderabad, Lucknow, Delhi, Bombay..." Apart from my own, India is the country I love most. When Peri told me weeks ago she was going, I began dreaming about India. It was a kind of homesickness.

19th October, Thursday. Leura.

Very hot. The lawn's been mowed. I see now it was a mistake to put daffodils through it because, until they have died off, they can't be cut or there will be no flowers next year. Nan had come over to give me advice on what to do down the side where roses and daisies grow, and it was clear she'd been surprised at the sight of the lawn blowing seeds in the wind. So the only thing was to mow around the bulbs.

Yesterday the school bus rushed past as I walked down to the gate on the look-out for Sam. He came up from behind, hot and cross. The bus driver had let him out where – as Sam put it – we go for bushwalks. He sat at the kitchen bench eating afternoon tea, muttering and looking dark. The drivers possibly don't know he's only six and has never been on buses alone before. I have told the morning driver but there are different men in the afternoons. The bus had stopped again for the driver to see his girlfriend. I am absolutely sure this is illegal, but I am reluctant to risk Sam being the one blamed for telling.

Lying in the sunroom we watch the bird cherries wave in the wind. They are coming into white bloom. Pines sway, the tall thin gum brushes the sky. Silence falls while I read.

Last night the world's oldest known woman, 120 years old, French, was on television. A gerontologist said she had lived so long because she had led all her life in a temperate climate, free from stress. He went on to say that soon many people will live as long as this. The old woman, serene and astute, although blind and half-deaf, when asked how she sees the future, replied "Short".

The philosophical and psychological problems and challenges of old age are the ones I'm interested in. I am now the oldest person in our family. It is an endless belt and when I first saw my grandson, I knew I had moved up towards the end. When my mother died at 93 last year, I knew it again.

On the living room wall are photographs of six generations of women. From Helen Jamieson (née Aiken) 1814-1901, then Helen Aiken Venn (née Jamieson) 1843-1919, to Helen Mary Dutton (née Venn) 1869-1957, to Gweneth Kate Llewellyn (née Dutton) 1897-1986, next to myself, to Lily. The clothes are interesting too. Ghilly saw Helen Mary Dutton laced into a velvet jacket and skirt and said "That's Violetta's costume." The first radical change in look is Gweneth Kate in a loose Twenties floral dress, the first with short bobbed hair. The others are corsetted and have enormously long hair in curls or crowns of plaits.

I am becoming increasingly aware of my own and my friends' ageing. I am finding it ludicrous and amazing that the girls I knew, who danced at balls in strapless dresses and long kid gloves, are old now. I have been photocopying a *Time* magazine article 'The oestrogen dilemma' for my friends. That's what it's come to. One minute you're belle of the ball. Next you're sending your friends articles on Hormone Replacement Therapy.

When I think of change, I think of a girl I trained with at the Royal Adelaide Hospital. Black hair, an Irish complexion, a beauty who wore a white linen dress to a wedding and a green straw hat. She gave me the hat. (It had a pleat in its brim and it was that that made it famous.) She was so lovely you laughed when you saw her. She married a doctor.

Twenty years later I saw her in a restaurant. She was on the telephone to a child of hers and finished by saying "Don't forget to ring me up!" I have never forgotten it, the contrast left me so astounded. It was not that it was unnatural, or odd at all. It was just because it was so natural that it seemed so remarkable. Men queued to dance with her but she had to ask her child to ring her.

20th October, Friday. Leura.

More heat. Yesterday had a sulky quality threatening storm when my neighbour Bill O'Connor gave me a lift to Katoomba. Yet there was no change and today it is still sullen and threatening, calm and hot but malevolent.

A bang at the screen door and a thump meant a parcel. It was a book from my cousin Rosemary Turner, *Stagecoach to Birdsville* by Helen Ferber. It is a history of some German families in South Australia. Two years ago Rosemary, her husband Peter, my brother Bill and I crossed the Simpson Desert. I didn't know the stoney wreck of Farina was where her family had lived from 1882. Together we walked around, climbed down into the underground bakery and felt the mournful quality of all such places.

Waiting for the school bus, as I am now, reminds me that I met Sam's headmistress today at St Cadice's. Because the bus pass was left at home, I took it to school. A modern nun greeted me wearing mufti. We chatted and she took the pass.

Later

Now, once again red and hot, Sam has stormed in. I asked what had happened.

"The driver wouldn't stop at our place."

"You must have had to cross the road then?"

"No I didn't."

Then as I turned and stood at the sink, he got off his stool where he was having afternoon tea and said

"Actually I've told you a lie. I got off at the lollipop shop."

"Why?"

"The bus was going on. It wasn't coming down the Mall."

Nan has even tried to trail the bus bringing Sam home in her car, stopping each time the bus did, but then when it veered off down Craigend Street she realised it was the wrong bus. She was trying to find out where the driver lets the children out to play while he meets his girlfriend. A new idea is to offer Sam twenty cents for each time he gets the right bus and gets out at the gate. In ten days he has only twice come home correctly.

The so-called nun has just rung. She is a mother of five. I had put that serene look down to the single life and the orderliness of the convent.

21st October, Saturday. Leura.

Mist rolled in like smoke through the heat. In the night it rained. It's quiet. Sam's gone to stay with his friend Jack Gorman for the weekend. I miss him.

Nasturtiums are coming up. The *Souvenir de la Malmaison* pink roses are sodden and turning to grey blotting paper. This is a rose with a problem. While it blooms profusely, damp sops it into balls that turn fawn and mouldy. It can have blush pink cabbage roses by the hundred in the sun or this horror. My friend Philippa, who has gone to live at Thirroul, said it was not the perfect rose for the mountains. But she kept hers. I asked my neighbour Cheryl Maddocks which she thinks are the best climbing roses for here. She said *Wedding Day* and *Crepuscule*.

The climbing *Peace* roses outside the bedrooms are budding. If I were planting roses now I would use almost all climbers. They have so many more flowers and take up no more soil space. The Anglican church burnt down about three years ago. Just smouldering walls and black rafters were left. Outside was a *Peace* rose that had been badly pruned a year before and had just recovered. I stood and cursed when I saw the pruning. I watched again as the scaffolding went up and the builders walked around the almost unnoticeable rose, burnt as it was back to a stump. Last week I saw it in full bloom, green swathes of branches half-covering the walls. It seems an emblem of faith and recovery.

Later

A few weeks ago I spent three hours looking for Susan Chadwick's letter about her breast cancer, and finally abandoned the search and wrote to Susan asking for a copy and permission to quote from it. When I first read it I cried. I hardly know if this rainy day I have the strength to quote it. But because it is brave, and full of information that may be useful, I will.

> Kate, on Feb. 24 I had a mastectomy and I am currently having chemotherapy for breast cancer. It all happened so quickly and my life has so totally changed in such a short time that there are

still friends like you whom I have not had the time to tell. About Feb. 14, I noticed that my left nipple was inverted and quickly went to a series of doctors all of whom thought it would be scar tissue from my breast reduction five years ago. Fortunately they and I were not satisfied until we had investigated further and as it turned out, my left breast had two large areas of cancer. [An operation showed] I had an "ordinary invasive breast cancer" 4.3 cms in size, fortunately with good margins. He [the surgeon] also removed seventeen lymph glands from under my arm and found seven to be positive. My cancer is a Stage 2. And I have had a number of other tests and thank goodness, have no secondaries in bones, lung or liver.

I thought I knew quite a bit about breast cancer but I didn't. It is a deadly disease with no cure. All breast cancer is considered systemic and 50% of women diagnosed are dead within five years, with an average life expectancy of 21 months. The other 50% live longer. How much longer? They can't tell me. They don't even collect the statistics because "breast cancer is usually found in women 55 plus and they are going to die of something in ten years or so anyway."

The chemotherapy helps only 10 out of 100 women who have it. Untreated, 60% of women die in five years. If the cancer is under two cms and none or fewer than four lymph glands are involved, the five-year survival rate goes up to about 70%. That's not my case of course but it shows you how appalling the prognosis is, even with small lumps discovered and removed early.

The medical profession doesn't generally believe in any of the adjuvant therapies and it is a No-Man's-Land of genuine help and quackery which you have to find your own way through, should you decide as I have, that you *can* make a difference and want to do all you can for yourself.

I have agreed to the chemo because I believe I am an exceptional patient and will come through this and live many years. I have become an expert on the subject of conventional and alternative treatments for it and feel very positive about my own outcome. As soon as I had the first mammogram I knew it was suspect and started on diet, intravenous vitamins etc. and have been following a rigid Vegan/Breast Cancer diet since then which was a week before surgery...

I think the cause of my cancer was stress, diet – particularly animal fats – hormones and genetics. (My dad's mother had a mastectomy in her sixties.)

And I think the way I will beat it will be a combination of medical and alternative methods... It's hard work but it's worth it to see Margaux grow up. I figure she needs me for a lot longer yet and I am not impressed with five and ten-year survival rates – I need to do a whole lot better than that...

I don't feel mutilated at all and in fact feel rather strong and proud to be like one of the Amazons who cut off their breast to make them better with the bow.

Now I call Susan 'Penthesilea', after the Amazon Queen.

No sooner had I finished quoting this letter than the women's show on radio began, on the very subject. Three years ago Anita Keating, Patron of the Breast Cancer Council, announced that 700 women a day are diagnosed with breast cancer in Australia. A woman who had a mastectomy forty-three years ago spoke. She is a volunteer in the Breast Cancer Support Society. So of course it is possible to survive in spite of the statistics.

"What is your best advice to give other women?" asked the interviewer.

"Just check your breasts and, if there's anything there you don't like, check with your GP."

It is National Breast Cancer Day on Monday.

I have spent hours searching for copies of Joseph Banks' letters. Writing to the gardeners on board the *Guardian*, the ship taking his specimens home to England, he begs and admonishes them to be careful.

The chief enemy to the health of plants in sea voyages is the salt spray which seldom fails to rise. Unless it is speedily washed off with freshwater the plant invariably dies.

Philippa is restoring the garden at Varroville, the home of her sister and brother-in-law. It was originally owned by Capt. and Mrs Charles Sturt. She has just sent me, from the *Life of Charles Sturt*, the story of their son almost drowning in the tear-shaped dam they made. This beautiful dam is still there half-full of waterlilies.

Turner, busy in the kitchen, was interrupted by his master's favourite retriever, who burst in upon him whining beseechingly, bounding to and from the door, and at last tugging at his clothes. Turner, following, saw the dog rush to the pond and dash into the water, and in an instant a bit of plaid upon the surface told him all. Another moment and he had pulled from the slimy water the unconscious child, whom he thought lifeless as he handed him to the nurse.

It goes on to say that the boy did live.

Captain Sturt on returning home heard on his threshold of the birth of one son and of the grave illness of the other, who then still lay between life and death.

The *Magnolia alba* I planted on the death of Alexis, Philippa's son, is in full bloom. Flowers like white doves, pale big green leaves sagging with raindrops. It took four years to begin to grow. At first it seemed useless, then suddenly up it went and bloomed soon afterwards.

I have not stepped out today, feeling locked in, although I could have gone for a walk in the mist. I washed the curtains and hung them by the fire.

Colette's husband locked her in for hours and would not let her out until she had written enough. Over and over writers express, in their diaries and letters, the wish to be left alone to work. Yet they very often conspire to be with people. Not always – but they are torn. The wish to be with friends and to be hospitable wars with the longing for solitude and work. Virginia Woolf is the best and most poignant example of this. She never solves the difficulty although she goes on longing right up to the end. Then she does the ultimate thing to ensure solitude.

Once a woman told me she was unable to write while her

family was at home, so she actually wrote on the lavatory. This seemed so abominable to me I asked if she couldn't get her family to allow her one hour a day utterly to herself to work. I have never had an answer but from time to time her poems are published in magazines and newspapers.

I am reading *Dirt, the Ecstatic Skin of the Earth* by William Bryant Logan. It's a collection of brilliant essays. The author says that he was always puzzled by the story of Moses and the burning bush. Until he realised that what Moses actually glimpsed out of the corner of his eye was reality. The bush was burning because all that is living burns. "This is a fundamental act of nature." We are flames.

22nd October, Sunday. Leura.

'Would that my love were in my arms and I in my bed again,' the Tallis scholars sang as I woke.

Outside the air smells of rain and jasmine. The jasmine flowers have climbed up the bare tree trunks between me and my neighbour Elizabeth. Two apple trees each have a branch weighed down with rain. Buds of apples are forming. This I think is the time when, if the temperature goes up, coddling moth infects the fruit.

As I got up from bed I saw the folder of Banks' letters beside the chest-of-drawers. These came from the University library at Lismore where, by good chance, I finally found them in a book published in 1982. It is comprised of letters to and from Banks, Governor William Bligh, Governor Phillip and others, on growing plants.

Sitting in the kitchen I was amazed to discover, in Banks' *Endeavour* Journal, a description of the same jelly fish that I saw washed up on the beach at Ballina. As long as I live I will never get over the astonishing way coincidences occur. This is from an entry made in April 1770.

> Calm again: I again went out in my small boat and shot much the same birds as yesterday; took up also chiefly the same animals to which was added indeed *Actinia natans*. I again saw undoubted

proofs that the Albatroses eat Holothurias or Portuguese men of War as the sea men call them. I had also an opportunity of observing the manner in which this animal stings. The body of it Consists of a bladder on the upper side of which is fixed a kind of Sail which he erects or depresses at pleasure; the edges of this he also at pleasure gathers in so as to make it Concave on one side and convex on the other, varying the concavity or convexity to which ever side he pleases for the conveniency of catching the wind, which moves him slowly upon the surface of the sea in any direction he pleases. Under the bladder hang down two kinds of strings, one smooth and transparent which are harmless, the other full of small round knobbs having much the appearance of small beads strung, these he contracts or extends sometimes to the length of 4 feet. Both these and the others are in this species of a lovely ultramarine blew, but the more common one which is many times larger than this being near as large as a Gooses egg, they are of a fine red. With these latter however he does his mischief, stinging or burning as it is called if touched by any substance: they immediately exert millions of exceeding fine white threads about a line in length which pierce the skin and adhere to it giving very acute pain.

The day before Banks had shot a Wandering Albatross and was intrigued when these stingers were disgorged, giving him his first proof that the albatross is immune to them.

A grey wattle bird flew up as I walked out to tip out the compost. Black cockatoos were calling in the mist.

At dusk yesterday my old friend Auckland rang from New Zealand. We talked for half an hour about our friends, our work, reviews and critics.

Then I read an interview with Harold Bloom, the critic, published in the *Paris Review*. I laughed out loud. He's wonderful. An original mind, audacious, brilliant, wise and passionate. He believes current French literary theory will not stay in vogue, because ultimately it is just boring. It has objectivity, but not subjectivity, and it is the latter he says the reader must have.

Harold Bloom (who is not to be confused with Allan Bloom of

The Closing of the American Mind, a critic whom he does not much admire) considers the question of 'why does it matter?' He says there must be some relation between the way we 'matter' and the way we read. He says we must answer the questions of good and bad, and how and why. We must answer the question of the relevancy of literature to our lives. Why it means one thing to us when we are one way, and another thing to us when we are another.

No critic, he says, will any longer consider why a work does, or does not, evoke great anguish in us. This is dismissed as subjectivity.

The 'School of Resentment', as he calls many of the current modes of examining reading, would naturally consider such matters and considerations ridiculously naive.

Auckland and I had spoken about how a bad review of one's work stays in the mind, pierces the heart. The good ones, he thinks, don't stay with us because we think of our own writing in this way. I think quite the opposite. We dismiss much praise, grateful though we may be, because it does not hurt us. We know how far we have fallen short of our own aims, how we wanted the work to be good and how low in comparison is our achievement. It is this which makes us so suspicious of praise and so wounded by criticism. What the criticism has uncovered is what we feared.

Of course, I can see it from the other side, too – I do some reviewing. I'm waiting for a cheque from a review.

Shaw said, "Reviewing has one advantage over suicide: in suicide you take it out on yourself; in reviewing you take it out on other people."

It's comforting to consider your scathing critics as 'taking it out' on you, perhaps even as jealous. For myself, I find it's best to try to believe the harshest are right. That's the only way you won't hate them and it's hate which does most damage.

   I must go down to the shops again, to the lovely mist and the rain. There's no milk and the day is closing in.

Vaughan Williams' *Sea Symphony* is playing and the black cockatoos are screaming like gulls outside the window.

It is artichoke season. I'm going to cook *Artichauts à la Barigoue*. Here is the recipe:

6 artichokes
1 onion, finely chopped
1 carrot, finely chopped
2 lettuces, finely shredded
1 handful finely shredded sorrel (or young spinach leaves)
2/3 cup dry white wine
2/3 cup chicken stock
juice of 1 lemon
bouquet garni, salt and pepper
2 tbsp olive oil

Wash artichokes and cut off stalks and tips. Rub with lemon juice and stand in cold water to which lemon juice has been added.

Fry carrot and onion in olive oil in a heavy casserole (or pan) until softened. Add herbs and then artichokes, leaves uppermost. Add salt and pepper. Cover with lettuce and sorrel. Cook gently for 12 minutes.

Pour in wine and stock. Cover and simmer for about 1 hour, by which time the sauce will be much reduced. Serve on a hot dish with the sauce poured over.

This can also be cooked in the oven after the initial frying. It's very good.

23rd October, Monday. Leura.

It's cold. A magpie and a currawong were the only birds in the garden when I threw out potato salad today. All the others have gone. Years ago Muriel Moody told me, when I remarked on the strange silence, that the birds do come back but they go to the valley to breed. And so it proved. So now when I notice the silence I do not fear something sinister.

Speaking of that it would be good to have a few frogs. They must have pure rainwater. My neighbour Betty has succeeded with stones, shade and a bowl. Frogs came in autumn to the oval. Sam and I heard them and we peered and crept around. There they were, dozens in the side drain, burping and glugging. Then one day they were gone. There was a film on the water like kerosene.

But we do have moss. Margaret Attwood told me, when she was staying with me, that we're lucky to have so much. She paused at the corner where moss grows near a big pine and admired it. Pollution kills moss. In Canada pollution, drifting in from the United States, is grim.

She and her husband are birdwatchers and came to see the bowerbird, and its bower which it builds nearby. We went to Jenolan Caves and did various other things. Then we went to see the bower and it was gone, utterly destroyed. I was aghast. The man turned to me and said "It doesn't matter. I had to wait years to see the world's smallest bird in Cuba. If we had been able to come and see the bowerbird on our first visit, it wouldn't have seemed right."

Since then the bird and the bower have come back. I have never known why the bower was so completely destroyed. Vandals, a dog or the bird itself, it's never been clear.

The pleasure of kindling the fire from last night's coals has become addictive. I will give time to poking and fanning when a match would work faster. It may be a longing for continuity. Perhaps it's a primitive way to try to delay death. It may be I just don't want to waste a match.

Sam managed the bus trip home yesterday. Today he is going to get the twenty cents if he gets the right bus and gets off at the gate.

When I saw Bill O'Connor outside his workshop garage and told him the skylights are in, he asked what the light is now like. I told him it felt like a church. He said, face shining into the sun, "Yes Kate, do you know that lovely thing in scripture 'God's wonderful light?'" He's going to look it up for me.

When I used to see Bill in hospital after an abdominal blockage (from which George Eliot died), I thought he would never be the same again, even though it looked as though he would live. When people are eighty or so, any blow to a pillar of their castle weakens the main structure and there is a chain reaction. But now Bill is painting roofs, cleaning out gutterings, pruning, being acolyte on Sundays, going to funerals, lugging bags of old clothes into St Vincent's, and so on. If anything he seems stronger.

It seems a miracle. But it may be his genes, character, faith or will. He was an orphan and is one of those people of whom Nancy Keesing would have asked "Tell me what went right?" She would have been glad that Bill doesn't belong to the 'culture of complaint' where everything is used as an excuse for misery. But Bill is up there with Albert Facey, whose biography *A Fortunate Life* Nancy was talking of at the time.

When I look down I see Lily's boots under the table. I am wearing them because she took my elastic-sided ones to New York.

Reading a New York cook book yesterday, I discovered that *schmalz* is rendered-down chicken fat. In a Jewish restaurant there called Sammy's, it is served in jugs for those with the craving. Stan Zimmerman is the owner of Sammy's (157 Chrystie Street at Delancey Street). Schmalz is mixed with 'gribeness' (the cracklings left over from making it), chopped liver, black radish and a bit of chopped onion, to make the Jewish Caesar salad the waiter tosses at the table.

An incredible change has come over what we consider safe to eat. Children after school once ate dripping on bread with salt and pepper (or sugar), which was about the same as pouring schmalz on bread.

Peri and I once went researching Jewish restaurants in Sydney. It was in the service of a Jewish lover of mine about to arrive from the USA. Later it turned out my friend didn't particularly care for Jewish food as he didn't consider it one of the world's great cuisines.

Reading this book I was overcome with an urge to get up and make chicken soup with a whole chicken. It's now believed to be really good for colds and not just a saying. It's called New York penicillin in the book. Everybody remembers soup at home and craves it occasionally. My mother's chicken soup was pretty good, but more German than Jewish. Whenever I went home this soup was on the stove ready. Lily wrote the recipe down. I can't find it but this is how I remember it:

> Boil either a chicken, or 2–3 cups of giblets, with 2 chopped onions, 2 cups of celery, 2 cups of pearl barley, salt and pepper. Chicken and the giblets make a better, more traditional soup. Start with cold water and boil until tender.
> Grate 2–3 cups of carrot into the soup. Reheat and serve. The grated carrot sweetens it and has a different taste altogether from chopped carrot. Sprinkle chopped parsley and taste for salt and pepper. The chicken meat left over can be used for sandwiches.

In the search for this leafing through an old book I found recipes from lunch parties we had when we shared recipes. The real purpose of the lunches was to talk to other young married women, but the device to start this off was to bring a favourite recipe. At first I was astounded to be reminded that I had ever spent my time so lightly. Now I saw that it was almost revolutionary of us to value each other in this way. There was so much going on to keep us apart and make us think it only important to be with men. Not that this was ever *said*. It was simply deeply understood. Women at lunch together in restaurants were put as much out of sight as possible. Ideally they were sent downstairs.

Also, in the searching a letter from my mother rose up.

Daughter,

I've just come back from Mavis's Cup Party. I won the sweep. I was always lucky – that's how I scooped the pool with your father.

I put in some old cauliflower seeds I'd saved and they went like fire up a cat's back. I've made apricot jam – a lot of it. Dr Harbison came out and I gave him some of last year's lot. When he climbed up to the top cupboard to get it out I gave him a cloth and he

cleaned the exhaust fan for me. Then he forgot to take my blood pressure. I wish I could send you a jar with this. Here's some cuttings from the *Bunyip*. Tucker's bought a ram – it cost $34,000. So here's a cheque for you. You're so poor and he's so rich I wish I could slice a bit from both of you. Here are some cauliflower seeds – just keep them watered and you'll have whoppers. Tell Lily not to marry that chap – it's no good when men don't respect women they take lovers and it doesn't make them happy for long – it makes them edgy, sly and unsatisfied with anyone. Men must respect women your father respected me you see. Girls nowadays have trouble with men because they sleep with them before they marry. It doesn't work! Now I've got to make a chocolate cake because Beck and neighbours are coming to bridge tomorrow. Here's the recipe.
Love Mum.
Don't waste the money-spend it on new guttering or a decent stove yours is a real old brute. Love Mum.

Frankly I find cooking meals daily harder than expected. I have lived alone so long I just make a large dish of something and eat until it's all gone. This is probably how people start on the path to malnutrition. First the chicken soup or beef stew, then just down to porridge. Then tea.

My own paternal grandmother, never a cook or much interested in food (being English, my mother said), ended up on bananas and tea for years. With just a piece of toast from time to time. Thin and sarcastic, she probably had berri-berri which makes people impatient in its early stages. But it could have been just her style. Never given to praise, she retreated to gentle mockery, her bed and a tray on her knees. Although the French windows let in the light from a garden hedged with *Lorraine Lee* roses, her room with its dark furniture seemed to a child elegant, cold and foreign.

On radio Margaret Throsby has asked Claudio Alcorso what now, in old age, he has to say about the kind of things that bring him happiness. Taken down incompletely, but as fast as I could, this is what he replied:

Society values economic rationalism. Happiness and the things that bring it are not entirely subject to this. I've had happiness when my daughter was born at dawn. I've had happiness walking, seeing the first leaves of the vines. It can be the laughter of a child. A kiss from someone you love. I've never thought of economic success as bringing happiness. It's other things that bring happiness.

He is eighty-two.

Later

It chokes me to think of Sam's vulnerability, the vulnerability of all children. I can't think about it. Rhythm and stability are what I'm trying to offer him.

On *The World's Funniest Video Show* the sight of children falling or being hurt is meant to be funny.

Babs rang from Adelaide. She's back from Spain. After a chat about her trip, I told her these are what I'm aiming for with Sam. She said, "Rhythm's important. It doesn't matter so much about the other." But I can't see how you can have one without the other. She told me she is going to Boston to wheel her daughter Fiona's baby in her pram outside the State Library (which is opposite where Fiona and her husband live). She added, "So this is my life now. I'll be spending three months with the baby."

This is the woman whose husband, Patrick, drank champagne from her shoe when they first met one New Year's Eve. A thing like that stays in a girl's mind. Some months later he bought her a pink ball gown in a white box. Their three daughters have kept that dress in that box.

The last meal I had with Patrick was at Cheong Liew's in Adelaide where we ate shark's lips and sea cucumber. Then, on holiday in Italy, he died and Babs brought him home for one of the biggest funerals the town's ever had. Once skiing, Caro dodged a tree, hit Patrick, knocked him out and stood there frozen, thinking she'd killed him. These two had the tenderest relationship. He used to say "Hello Caro" in the most curiously loving way. We are all lucky we knew him. I still miss him.

24th October, Tuesday. Leura.

Last night Lily rang from New York. She said she wanted to talk to Sam who was asleep. I ran down the hall, tried to wake him, picked him up, something I can't do normally, and ran back to the phone. Once there I clapped the phone to his ear. He groaned in his sleep. Not once did he open his eyes while his mother sang out her love for him over the distance. Finally, when I thought enough time had passed, I took the phone from him to speak myself. He slid from my lap onto the couch and lay there. While I was carrying him back to bed he suddenly opened his eyes and said "Mum must be very worried about me."

This morning he remembers nothing. So we went over the call with me playing his mother's role, talking about visiting the world's biggest toy shop and asking him to guess what might be in her laden arms as she emerged.

"Something with a battery in it," I suggested.

"A remote control car?"

"Maybe."

Uproar here. Suzie, a professional cleaner, has come. Now piles of china are in bags with old woks, ready to throw out. She said, as I was throwing out the rhododendrons dying in the hall, "You'll have an empty house soon."

Once my friend Julia, who was the first true example of an intellectual woman I ever met, stood before a wall of built-in wardrobes, the sea pounding outside the floor-to-ceiling windows, the Steinway grand piano in one corner and a mass of clothes on the floor thigh-high. She looked beaten. When I asked her what she was doing, she said "My aim is to get the clothes into the wardrobe." This still makes me laugh.

My aim is to be able to walk through the house without treading on anything other than the floor or a mat.

Opening a drawer, hoping to lighten its load, I found a white dress I last wore running up the steps of Meikles Hotel in Zimbabwe last year. The man who had dropped me off there said, as I turned back to hear, "A word of advice. That dress needs a slip." With a stone in my heart I knew this affair would be short.

One more word on the domestic. It is incredible but I know, from the way the sink looks, that inside the cupboards are clean. How it is that closed doors and a polished sink reveal this quiet knowledge, I don't know. But it is so. Squalor is depressing. Cleanliness uplifting. I ought to have had a cleaner years ago.

My mother used to be distressed, after visiting her mother in her great old age, because there were blue marks on the walls around the brass light switches. Granny couldn't see that when she polished she'd left stains. Failing eyesight makes elderly people seem daft or as if they've lost energy or style, when the truth is merely that they can't see as well as they once did. Wearing spectacles while washing-up may be useful but it's not a thing that comes naturally.

Suzie, this small red-haired woman who is so energetic, has found a real silver teapot. I said I would buy something special if Silvo wasn't good enough. She said, quietly and intensely, "You already have the best silver cleaner in the world." Was it herself? Or myself if I rubbed hard enough? "This," she said, waving a black tube of car chrome polish in the air. It came from the time Hugh had a racing car, and has been in the cupboard ever since. "This is my professional secret" she said. Not after this it isn't.

The teapot is Caro's, left to her by her great aunt Mollie Dutton. How many cups of tea this pot has poured for all those sisters-in-charge of the great wards of the Royal Adelaide Hospital. The weekly games of Canasta in their retirement. The years of friendship before. These were the women who, with the power of empresses, ran the wards where my friends and I trained.

Some of these Sisters spent twenty years or more in charge of the same ward. It was a mistaken practice because it led to them becoming so inflexible, so vain in some cases, so power-drunk under their starched modest bonnets, they were as dangerous as South American dictators. There were noble exceptions but the system was terrible.

Many of these Sisters were riddled with opinion, irritability and petty power. There were some who often behaved like drunken sailors on the first night ashore. There were some who did not physically touch another person from one year's end to another. Often they lived the lives of nuns, with none of the strengthening meditation and support of a religious vocation. Vocation many had, but with little education and few restraints, they were left to rule as despots with whatever vagary of cruelty or compassion possessed them that day. It is strange that the wards in which humanity and gentleness were meant to be flourishing were ruled in that way. As in all things there were memorable exceptions, but vicious treatment, witnessed or experienced, is hard to forget, especially if at the time you had to remain polite and humble.

As for the doctors, they lived in another realm. As planets pass through the sky, they moved through the wards, flipping over notes, asking the odd question, hooking a stethoscope into an ear, prodding it over a fat chest here or thin rattling chest there. Finally it was lodged in the breast pocket and left to hang round the neck, like two question marks on the meaning of life. It was hard to feel sympathy for even the students and house doctors, plagued though they were by the imperiousness of honorary physicians and surgeons, who were as remote as suns and moons from the ordinary life of the wards.

These senior men had been injected on arrival with the virus the entire system was dedicated to raising to plague proportions. Naturally then they were often brutish to their juniors, mocking, savage and ruthless. I am told things have changed but I wonder.

When I was nursing and Aunt Mollie retired – and I am not trying to link her in any way with these sisters and doctors – I bought her a frangipani plant in a pot. It stuck out like a brown thumb from the soil. I carried it on the bus to her house. This new house of hers had been built next to her sister's. There it was intended that Mollie would nurse her sister's son for the rest of his life. He was a sailor with polio, about to come out of hospital. I married him.

The frangipani grew into a tree higher than the house. I don't know why I chose that for her. I knew nothing of gardens except geraniums, but she gardened. I suppose the plant caught my eye because of its pretty label.

But I also saw a lot of kindness when I first began training at a country hospital. I remember the young Sister Sharpen who used to say, shivering, wrapping her red cardigan round her white uniform tightly on cold nights, "Night Duty, thy name is cruelty". She was the one who I wanted most to be like. And I remember the GP, who is now a psychiatrist, with whom I correspond. Recently I wrote to him about a sixteen-year-old girl who was brought into theatre dead on arrival.

Sister Mac and I laid her out. I did not know why she was not in the morgue. I thought perhaps others were there from the accident, so it was too full. I was crying, but Sister Mac kept calmly on while I sobbed and helped. The girl was so perfect, no mark on her body from the car accident. She had a Bandaid on her toe, that was her only imperfection. I thought that as she wrapped her toe she did not know we would be the ones who saw it.

Sister Mac folded the girl's arms across her chest like a saint. The other Sisters placed the arms down beside a person. That was, I thought, because they weren't Catholic as Mac was.

This in part is what the psychiatrist wrote in reply:

...in your letter about the girl in that operating theatre of the hospital. I had carried her from the back seat of my old Standard Vanguard and put her on the operating table. God knows why, because the poor girl had a broken neck. The police asked me to go to the scene of an accident on the Lyndoch road near the old Sandy Creek School. There were three of them in an old Landrover. The driver was a young man and he failed to take the left-hand corner before the school. They were all lying on the road being attended by Mary's sister and brother-in-law Glen Maguire, who were returning to Gawler for a holiday. Between us we thought that the sixteen-year-old was in urgent need of care, as she was comatose with stertorous breathing, and rather than wait for the ambulance to arrive we bundled her into the back seat of my car and I drove alone to the Hutch, listening to her laboured breathing changing its rhythm, and wondering what we should do with her when we got there.

It is interesting how you have kept in touch with those four and how they have kept in touch with each other. They were a very special group of women and I feel privileged to have known them. They exhibited a special brand of competence, efficiency and experience that made my beginning in General Practice less lethal – but I really did find that experience particularly stressful because there was always something happening – like that girl's death, when you wondered if you had handled it differently, she might not have died.

Like another case we share of that girl with the mass in her abdomen who developed peritonitis and adhesions and lingered for a month on a drip with antibiotics and good nursing. That experience ripped my guts out. Thinking about it still hurts …

The shadow of Gawler days still hangs heavily on my shoulders as we were not trained sufficiently to handle all that was thrown at us. Like tying bleeders in tonsillar fossae in the middle of the night when Hans or Sharpen or Mac would ring and say "One of your tonsils is bleeding". Now nursing doesn't cater for the fresh-faced young women who were a joy to work with and whose patients fell in love with them. The Roseworthy College boys queued in droves to take them out and were grateful for a kiss …

25th October, Wednesday. Leura.

Serenity rules. A red king parrot was sitting among the white cherry blossom which had fallen to the ground. I watched it from the bath. These parrots love the seeds, like dry Weetbix crumbs, which drift in from the beech trees lining the street. The paths are thick with them now, and children run and toss them up over each other, whirling, bending, throwing.

I went to town and gave out the prizes for the women's poetry and prose competition at Sydney University. At one end of a big room there was a long table covered with a white cloth and cocktail food. Around this people sat like wallflowers at a ball. I joined them. After a while a convenor came over, handed me the envelopes with the cheques in them and made a short speech. I did my part. Then one of the joint winners of the prose prize came to speak to me and introduced her parents. Her mother said that she herself worked as a GP.

The young woman had earlier stood beside me chatting to a friend. She had suddenly tripped and fallen softly down like a wall of foam bricks. It was the most curious fall. It was as if she had no weight. Dark-haired, pale-skinned, she was wearing a black chiffon skirt and a beautiful grey wispy top made from a scrap of silk. At her neck was a lozenge of moonstone on a thin chain. She was lovely, a face like a pansy. She reminded me of the girl who had given me the green straw hat.

Her story had been about slashing herself with a razor blade after a relationship with a suicidal blackmailer. This is not all that uncommon. She showed me the inside of her arms when I said "Let me see your scars." She turned her hands outwards and there were the red streaks like pencil marks.

Her boyfriend walked beside me as I left with the family group – parents, young brother. He told me he was interested in making a film about scars. I asked the girl what she would do with the prize money (which was substantial). A book on tattoos and scars was what she had in mind. The more I heard, the more alarmed I became.

Later, her father drove me to Central Station.

"And what do you think of this?" I asked.

"I don't have an opinion. I don't get involved with these things."

Into the train, just before it left, stepped a huge youth with a half-shaved head and a pony-tail. "Somebody's always taking my seat," he shouted, as he pulled the seat back in front of me. When he took off his shoes the smell of his neglect spread around. I got up and went to the next carriage. My neighbours, Bill and Betty, think nothing of returning by train at one in the morning, but I am not keen and have only come back once or twice in the dark. Writing is thought to be one of the glamour jobs of the last two or three decades. I greet that idea with a hollow laugh.

The smell here now is from the robinia, the blossom of Nan's pink wisteria, the rose geranium I snatched from a fence and the port wine magnolia I got the same way.

Nan was having her garden inspected by Peta from the Open Garden Scheme. As I walked down her drive I found the two women peering at some aquilegeas, also called columbines. "Columba, columbine," said Peta. "It means a flock of birds. See how they are gathered round with their necks outstretched, drinking from a bowl?" I looked and looked and suddenly saw the petals *are* the backs of birds if you hold the flower upside down. Their necks curve up and inwards as if drinking in a circle. There's a dark blue flowerhead here on the table.

This morning at 8.30 Kathy, from Megalong Books, drove me to the Hydro Majestic Hotel to give a talk. Margaret Whitlam was leading a large group of about a hundred from John Willing's International Study Group.

The hotel has been revamped, and I've chosen the word carefully. Gold pelmets over every curtain. A colossal, multi-coloured racehorse toy in the vestibule – it's Melbourne Cup Week soon. We lugged in the boxes of books for sale, laid them out on a table and saw the view of the valley spread before us for hundreds of miles.

A woman began to weep while she was talking to me. She felt a book of mine had been written for her. When she read it, her husband had just left after 34 years, so it was her sadness that drew her to it. She said she was waiting for something to happen in the book. That was a wonderful comment, so grave. Because nothing *does* happen. It's like life. While we wait for the big events, we live. Living makes life, not great events.

But meals are being made all the time, gardens are being planted and fires lit. Friends visit. Somebody bakes a cake. It's

Christmas again. Now it's Easter, and someone paints the blown hen eggs. The washing dries on a tree. A house is sold.

It begins again. A child is born. People fall in love. A church bell tolls. A cash register rings and the milk is carried home. A child cries all night with earache. A period is missed, one heart quickens and another grows heavy. Homework gets done. The phone rings, the kettle whistles, and there's a divorce.

The moon waxes and wanes. Occasionally somebody looks up at it and sighs, tugs the blankets back around and goes to sleep. A dog barks and it's dawn. Roosters have been crowing for two hours. We wake and begin again.

Sam stayed with his friend Jack Gorman last night. Now I am waiting to see if he will manage the bus trip from school.

Later

"I've got a very very very wobbly tooth," Sam said, coming in through the gate, talking gingerly, hardly moving his lips. He asked me to pull it out, so I did. I almost fainted and I think he was close to it too.

There are two wedgetail eagle chicks in a nest of sticks in a photograph taken by my nephew, Angas, standing on his father's ute. (Anne, his mother, enclosed it in her letter which I got today. She also sent a photograph of my brother Tucker dressed in his green clothes, arms full of wildflowers, striding towards the camera looking as comfortable and pleased as he would be carrying a string of fish.) The chicks are covered with white fluff and have black eyes. Bits of red meat are hung about the nest like red petticoats on a washing line. Above there's only the blue sky. Imagine the feeling of a creature which never has anything above it apart from a parent from the time it first opens its eyes until it learns to dive.

26th October, Thursday. Leura.

Reading *The Tale of Squirrel Nutkin* in bed this morning made me see again how great a writer Beatrix Potter is. Words, as perfectly placed as tiles in a floor, pave the page, strong and irredeemable as concrete. When it comes to rhythm she can't be matched.

In the middle of the lake there is an island covered with trees and nut bushes; and amongst those trees stands a hollow oak-tree, which is the house of an old owl who is called Old Brown.

One autumn when the nuts were ripe, and the leaves on the hazel bushes were golden and green – Nutkin and Twindleberry and all the other little squirrels came out of the wood, and down to the edge of the lake.

They made little rafts out of twigs, and then paddled away over the water to Owl Island to gather nuts.

Each squirrel had a little sack and a large oar, and spread out his tail for a sail.

They also took with them an offering of three fat mice as a present for Old Brown, and put them upon his door-step.

I could go on all day.

In the film *Heartburn* Jack Nicholson, in a great scene, is reading *Jemima Puddleduck* to his daughter. Having heard his creaky voice rolling on and on, it's now impossible to read it without hearing him.

Later in the morning, at the supermarket, I asked Nan whether she liked Beatrix Potter. She told me how her daughter Anthea, when very young, sat on the stairs one day reading *Peter Rabbit* out loud. She and Phil crept down behind her, thinking how amazing it was that she could read so perfectly. The book was upside-down and she was reciting it. I thought of Phil, on submarines in the Atlantic for five years of the war.

My theory is, plunge the young into Beatrix Potter. At least they will be gripped, as the adult reading to them must be too. These 'Dot', 'Run!' and 'Why?' books are no fun.

I thought the story of *Pig Robinson* was her last. I'd felt she was on the verge of breaking out and writing something really wild. I was wrong. Graham Greene, writing about her work, says this tale was the first. Miss Potter had written him a short, sharp letter pointing this out when he had made my mistake in a review.

I have spent an hour looking for this with no luck. It drives me mad. Papers galore and I can never find anything I need.

As in other things in life, it is only when you abandon wanting something with great ardour that it materialises. When you turn away to other things or people, then it is that the object of desire touches you and says "Here I am." And you say "Where were you when I wanted you?" It is as if you set up a force to counter the strength and power of your longing.

Looking at the ceiling from the couch this afternoon, I noticed the light fittings draped with dusty cobwebs and remembered Betty O'Connor coming in after I had cleaned them once.

"Praise Mary Mother of God you've cleaned the lights!"

I was very charmed by this, wondering how long she had wished I would clean them and held her tongue. I was also struck because it was such a typically Catholic thing to say. An Anglican doesn't feel the need for an interceder and goes directly, perhaps brazenly, to God. Anglicans seem less in awe and don't involve Mary, or for that matter praise her.

Betty rings the doorbell as I am remembering this. She's come to invite us over for dinner.

27th October, Friday. Leura.

A picnic. The sun's come out gold from a grey silk sheet, the leg of some voluptuous beauty we'll never meet. Luciano Pavarotti is singing 'I don't love you'. I should, but don't, know the Italian title of this song.

There's a man for you. Waking at around 10 a.m., after a night of opera, supper – that kind of night – he's knotting his tie, singing into the mirror, late for work but off to be shaved by the barber. Greeting the day with total equanimity.

A dish of potatoes 'Jansson's Temptation' is in the oven to take with us when it's done. It's an old recipe, often found in books. It mainly consists of shredded potatoes and sliced onions. A few anchovies are slipped in between the layers. Cream is poured over the top and it's dotted with butter. It's baked gently for an hour.

Then thicker cream is added, a little salt and a fair bit of pepper. An odd dish to take to a man, Phil, about to have a heart operation. But one grows very tired of virtue. And whatever has happened to our hearts by now, a single dish with lots of cream in it won't make that much difference.

I am also baking a dish of about three kilos of Roma tomatoes, halved, put cut-side up and drizzled with olive oil. This hasn't got a name – just roasted tomatoes. It is good hot or cold, and makes a good base for chutney. The roasting concentrates the flavour. Cheap ripe tomatoes can be used. Did you know the reason tomatoes are used so much in sauces and as flavour-enhancers is that they have a lot of monosodium glutamate in them?

I began to taste the potato dish by dipping in some Turkish *labna* bread. And couldn't stop. And now a third's gone and it's too late to make more.

30th October, Monday. Leura.

Missed the bus, then missed the next one too. So Phil drove Sam to school, backing out the car like an aircraft carrier from a wharf.

A perfect summer day. King parrots flew ahead of us as we ran to the gate. Bees were all we heard as we sat on the seat waiting for the bus we'd already missed.

Tomorrow Lily comes home. She rang from London yesterday where she's staying with her sister Caro. I spoke to them both. I fall into a queer stoical cheerful tone talking to my girls long distance. But put down the phone and cried. Lily said she'd managed to get a flight four days early. Sam and I go over and over what we will do to greet her. Lying in bed, he runs over the scene again. Should he come to the gate to meet her? Or hide inside?

When Sam dreamt he was sunk to the bottom of the sea by a huge wave, Ghilly's husband John, who is a children's psychiatrist, said it is more likely fear of being swamped by his emotions, than it is sheer longing for his mother (as I had thought).

Hugh and Cathy spent Saturday night here. The four of us lay on their bed and tried to see the baby moving in her stomach. Each time she tried to catch the moment for us, it stopped just as we looked. We put our hands over the spot but waited to no avail.

Silence has fallen. I am waiting for Jack from Canberra. He is going to stay overnight. When a marriage ends, shards lie everywhere, dangerous and painful to everybody. It is hard to be honest and useful to both people when you have been with them both throughout their marriage. Blame is useless but it's there, under the table, like a hand-grenade.

31st October, Tuesday. Leura.

Jack arrived yesterday. He was grey with anguish.

I remember when our friend Woolfie was distraught, Hampton said that it was very hard for people suffering the appalling grief that comes from break-ups to believe that they, in six months time, are likely to be quite different. She meant they will probably be able to laugh and feel almost, if not entirely, well. But you can't say this to a person who is sitting there like a crushed snail.

I cooked while he sat on a stool watching.

This morning, I came out of a shop with a bottle of wine, Farnese. He recognised it and reminded me how once, in Tuscany, he and I visited a winery and tasted the new vintage. It was that wine, Farnese.

This was in happier times in another country and besides this marriage is dead.

We walked along arm-in-arm, with Sam swinging a stick, hitting the tops of the grasses. Black parrots screamed overhead like Messerschmitts. The grey fog trailed us round the streets.

We met Lily at the gate. She had not slept for three days. Rings under her eyes like truck tyres.

November

1st November, Wednesday. Leura.

Now Lily's home, the house is full of laughter like bells and the smell of Jean-Paul Gaultier. She's howling with laughter on the phone at this moment. Black clothes and new boots, presents and New York magazines lie around. It is as if the world's been given a couple of fast spins.

2nd November, Thursday. Leura.

Lily and I walked through the bush to Katoomba yesterday after Jack had left to go back to Canberra. We decided to drive down next week to stay with him.

A hot wind this morning. It seems like heart attack weather. I don't know why I think of this whenever it's hot, sultry and windy.

Nina Simone is singing 'I loves you Porgy', while Lily dances with Sam, singing to him.

Robert Lowell's face, smiling out of his striped shirt, stares up at me like a benevolent country parson, from the cover of his *Selected Poems*. This is what he writes of his parents, at the end of *During fever* :

> *Terrible that old life of decency*
> *without unseemly intimacy*
> *or quarrels, when the unemancipated woman*
> *still had her Freudian papa and maids!*

It comes at you out of the blue, right from his heart, like a loaf from the oven.

This morning I was interviewed on the phone by a travel journalist. I tried to be interesting – until my arm ached. I told him that the childhood my brothers and I lived had been one long holiday, interrupted by visits to grandparents, running as we did half-naked on a chalk-white yawn of a beach edged by white daisy bushes. What he will make of this I don't know.

This hot wind is getting me down. I must lighten up. We've got people coming to dinner. A rare event. There was a time in my life I had as many meals at home with guests as with the family. Now it's no more often than once every three months or so. I got sick of washing-up I suppose. People sometimes do get tired of work they once did willingly. My mother said she was worn out from sewing. So she stopped. No more pants for my brothers. No more dresses for me. Quite suddenly.

3rd November, Friday. Leura.

Arm-in-arm Nan and Phil walked across the black road after dinner last night, out under the arbour of white roses at the gate. The moon shone down like a white rose. Lily said as we watched, "See Mum, you could have that too. You don't have to think of it as a trap." But although I admire some marriages, I don't think it's for me. It is just too late.

The heat has blown the roses – *Madame Alfred Hillier*, *Peace*, *Madame Able Chattenay* and an unknown white bloom – so I brought in a bunch for the house. That great gouty blow of a red red rose, *President Lincoln*, is here, layered like a cake. The size of a man's fist, a stem like an erection. It is a red exultation. Courtesan or prize fighter, it wins the day. Phil brought it to Lily last night saying "I hope your mother won't be jealous. I've only got one. I've been waiting for it to come out." The perfume's a knockout.

The house is empty. Lily and Sam have gone to Sydney for the weekend.

Warwick, the new baker up the street, sells olive bread, which we had for lunch with the last of the rare roast beef Lily cooked for dinner. These new breads, made from organic flour with eleven per cent protein or more, are good.

Michael Ignatieff is writing in the *New York Review of Books* on Yugoslavia and points out that Tito is buried in a greenhouse with leaks in the glass roof dripping now onto the marble slab. He says that Tito was one of the very few Communist leaders who managed to unite people.

Try as I may the complexities of the former Yugoslavia are beyond me. At the moment my friend Ianesco and his partner Mirna, who is Croatian, are on their way there so that she can see her mother. This seems dangerous to me but perhaps that's how little I understand. Hugh's best man's brother Marko has videos of himself riding on the front of a Serbian tank, taken a few months ago. Hugh said "But Marko, that man with the bad haircut Milozovich is a war criminal." Marko said, "That's just a UN plot Hugh." Marko, a lawyer, says that at present he is a housepainter by day and rearranges the borders of Europe by night. Possibly true.

Dr. H. V. Evatt, writing his MA thesis in politics eighty years ago, said:

> Even in this year of grace 1917, there does not appear to be a general recognition that the actions of our leaders in social and political life should be guided by principle and not by expediency and necessity.

A beautiful family recollection was written by Michael Ignatieff. It was published in *Granta* in 1984. That seems an age ago. Now to find it. Here it is in Number 14, the autobiography issue. It's called 'August in my father's house.' It opens in the holiday house in the French countryside, which his ex-Russian diplomat father and Canadian mother have just bought.

It is after midnight. They are all in bed except me. I have been waiting for the rain to come. A shutter bangs against the kitchen wall and a rivulet of sand trickles from the adobe wall in the long room where I sit. The lamp above my head twirls in the draught. Through the poplars, the forks of light plunge into the flanks of the mountains and for an instant the ribbed gullies stand out like skeletons under a sheet.

Upstairs I can hear my mother and father turn heavily in their sleep. Downstairs our baby calls out from the bottom of a dream. What can his dreams be about? I smooth his blanket. His lips pucker, his eyes quiver beneath their lashes.

I have been married seven years. She is asleep next door, the little roof of a book perched on her chest. The light by the bed is still on. Her shoulders against the sheet are dark apricot. She does not stir as I pass.

And so it goes on, a simple account of a few days and of a life-time of memories.

4th November, Saturday. Leura.

Rain, snails and silence. Free to sleep in, I woke at 5.30 and read the papers.

I noticed a sick rhodendron down the lane yesterday. I gave it three buckets of water, two with a spoon of Thrive in them. Once a rhododendron begins to droop, it is one of the hardest things in the world to save. Sometimes I wonder if nematodes are eating the roots. Suddenly another thriving shrub slumps, in line with the gaps where others have already collapsed. I have tried transplanting others into new rich wet earth. No luck. It's a mystery and I am flummoxed. Another bucket this morning and, even with the rain, no change is visible. I wonder if I could save it if I dig it up, wash the roots and transplant it? Or will this kill it?

Gardening is like nursing. Suddenly, overnight, something collapses. Hasty pumping of fluids, close observation, experts called in. Death or recovery the outcome. And the continual feeling of helplessness and being beaten when death comes.

Behind the stone wall is a tall pine hedge and I wonder if its roots are throttling the shrubs. I'd like to cut that hedge back but it's not mine.

After lugging the buckets, I lay down with a hot water bottle. Opening, by chance, the *London Review of Books*, I came across an article 'Oh my aching back', a review of *The History of Pain* by Roselyne Rey. The reviewer quotes Rey:

> Pain remains poorly understood because it has no clearly defined status; all divisions between 'real' and 'subjective' pain, having been founded on archaic metaphysical mind/body dualisms, are plainly problematic, not to say question-begging. No physician can pop a thermometer into the brain or x-ray the heart. Whatever its nature or function, pain is *felt* [my emphasis].

Apart from the not unimportant fact that people may be addicted to pain-soothers, there never has seemed much point to me in trying to decipher what a person really is feeling. If someone says it hurts, that ought to be enough.

A woman called Elsie was my first experience of somebody inexplicably lying in bed, saying she was in pain and could not get up. She was a spinster of about fifty and because of this, it seemed to me, she was viewed as an hysteric. (This was in the little country hospital where I began nursing training.) I think it didn't matter if she could walk or not. A few aspirins and some decency, rest in bed and kindness, might not have gone astray. Calling her more or less a liar to her face and forcing her up, seemed brutal and besides there's always the awful possibility of wrong diagnosis. So Elsie was discharged and sent home in disgrace. But the disgrace I think was ours.

5th November, Sunday. Leura.

Every tree stretches to the blue sky, as if yawning after a good night's sleep. I walked for an hour thinking it's incredible that I landed here.

Marisa rang from Adelaide and told me she's going on a picnic with Phil, her husband, and Jack who is visiting them. I asked her what she was making.

"Fried eggplant with a Japanese dressing of mirin, sesame seeds, garlic, lemon and shoyu sauce. And fresh flat green beans, cooked, and lima beans. Also potatoes with a pesto that has no cheese in it. Just the basil, oil and nuts. Zucchini with a Moroccan pumpkin dip made with chilli, caraway and saffron. I'm rolling out a pizza dough as a pie casing, with a filling of cauliflower, dried tomatoes, red capsicum and olives, stewed. This one I'm doing in a tin but sometimes I make it like a folded *calzone.*"

"What's that?" I asked.

"*Calzone* means trousers. It's a sort of pasty."

"Oh yes. I remember having it in Assisi in a café. Maybe the trousers are the pastry and the leg is the filling."

"I don't know. I haven't looked it up."

She then went on with the menu. "A ricotta and spinach pie with pine nuts, and not just spinach, but greens, endive, chicory, and so on, in an oil pastry."

I went out to the kitchen and made a cold chicken sandwich with chutney.

6th November, Monday. Leura.

High fast bright clouds. The fire's lit. Lily's got a cold. Whooping like a troll in a cave in the night. It's her childhood over again. I am off to buy chicken for noodle soup.

Later

A day soaked in chicken noodle soup. Sam, sitting with a bowl on his knee as I interrupted him, said "Don't. I'm eating bizgetti."

People are getting ready for Cup parties. All except us.

Nan and I went to K-Mart and, peering into the deep freeze wells, she showed me frozen snacks. I bought pastizzi because it reminded me of Marisa's picnic menu even though that was one of the few things not on it. It's suddenly become clear to me that there's no longer any need to cook anything, unless you feel like it. All you need to do is put frozen things into the oven. Where have I been the last twenty years? I intend to modernise.

13th November, Monday. Canberra.

We came here, Lily, Sam and I, last Wednesday and stayed with Jack. On Friday Lily and Sam left to drive to Adelaide, to see her father who is ill with post-polio syndrome. He's now having trouble breathing, which he was at the time I met him.
People have gone to work. The suburbs have almost emptied. In the houses cleaners are at work. A car drives by. This computer hums. The wind ruffles the ivy on the trunk of the birch at the window. A child late for school plods past.
There's been no writing done because I've been in bed. I've had flu. I got up once and walked around a lake with Jack, while we talked about his life. The lake lay there like a blue eye staring at the equally blue sky. Formidable grief, like his at the end of a marriage, will take some getting over. Even a walk takes him effort. But then so does sitting still. The grief is like a whining dog that rarely lets him be. While we sat watching Lily shell green prawns for dinner, we talked and laughed and he said he felt almost euphoric. But grief is always standing there at the door, waiting to take him prisoner again.
We are often helped in our lives by the knowledge that we are surrounded by people who have come through common experiences. With child-birth, for example, it is encouraging to look around and realise that so many have accomplished it with serenity, or at least success. Even though it still seems so enormous a task the first time, one wonders that anybody can survive it and remain sane. When I was pregnant, every time I looked at a street full of people I'd think that if so many had managed this, I might too. But I was full of doubt.
It is amusing that exactly the opposite can happen, as with love-making when you are young. I used to believe, truly believe, that we were the first people who ever invented these acts. I would look around a bus, as it took me to the city, and think 'If these people knew what I have been doing, they would be astounded.' It simply did not occur to me that they could ever have done the same. No, these were our acts, ours alone. We were the

geniuses who had made these inventions. Nobody ever had, nobody ever possibly could, reach the same heights. Titans, we towered over the world as lovers. I think this is not an uncommon feeling in the innocent. It is a form of grace perhaps.

Christie and Robert asked us to dinner last night. They suggested to Jack what he might try to see when he goes to Jordan next month, on a trip to co-ordinate an art exhibition, a joint showing of Palestinian, Israeli and Australian painters. They got out books of photographs of Petra.

Christie asked if we'd like to go to a lecture on philosophy for children next Thursday. I am going to take Clare, Rosie and Jack's ten-year-old daughter. I want to hear John Passmore talk because often, when Sam and I discuss our shadows or our souls or God, I am tangled and stumble over these insubstantial but not unimportant matters. Where does the soul reside? In your eye? I say it's in the head, but it could be the ear for all I know. He accepts my answers to his questions in his quiet way, but then asks something harder. He says he doesn't believe in God, but prays for his father and our neighbour.

"Why, Phil?"

"Because he's going to have an operation."

Sam's is, I think, the position of a great number of people – doubting like a true believer.

I've been laughing reading what I think is the first ever *Paris Review* book of interviews. There's one with James Thurber. He started by giving a long history of the bloodhound, and the interviewer had a hard job getting him off the subject.

Then he said that he did not see his drawings as art because he did them so quickly. He added that they don't always come out the way he intends.One, for the *New Yorker*, had a naked woman on all fours on top of a bookcase, high up near the ceiling. Below her in the room are her husband and two other women. The husband is saying to one of them "This is the present Mrs Harris. That's my first wife up there." He had meant the naked wife to be at the top of a staircase, but had accidentally drawn the bookcase.

The *New Yorker* editor, Harold Roos, was confused, having a literal-minded and grim approach to this, as to all humorous writing. He asked Thurber if the woman on top of the bookcase was supposed to be alive, stuffed or dead. Thurber replied "I don't know, but I'll let you know in a couple of hours." Calling back he told him he'd talked to a taxidermist, who'd said you can't stuff a woman, and to his doctor who'd told him a dead woman cannot support herself on all fours.

"So Roos," he said, "she must be alive."

"Well then, what's she doing up there naked in the home of her husband's second wife?"

Thurber said, "You have me there."

I once gave my students a great piece of writing on Thurber, also published in the *New Yorker*. But it left them puzzled. My focus was not on Thurber, but on the piece of writing about him, which was itself so beautiful. But I failed to make this clear. I find it amazing that I try to teach people about writing. My main aim is to do no harm. Sometimes I think this is possible. So many are given talent, lashings of glorious, fabulous talent. But few choose to use it.

I met one of my ex-students, Isobel, at the Opera House selling tickets, and asked what had happened to her story. She said she had been too busy earning a living to take her writing further. That woman can write. She also needs to keep herself. I could wring my hands to see her doing anything else but writing. Time's a-flying.

After coming across the interview with Thurber, I discovered, in the same issue, some strange facts about writers' superstitions. Truman Capote has lots. To be able to write he cannot have any yellow roses around, although they are his favourite flowers. He will neither travel on a plane with three nuns, nor have three cigarette butts in the ashtray. He won't begin writing, and he won't end, on a Friday. And so on. Rudyard Kipling, when writing, had to placate a daemon that only drank black ink. He said he would have ideally kept an ink-boy to grind Indian ink. Blue-black was an abomination.

Willa Cather read the Bible before writing, not from piety but because she hoped to be affected by the prose. She wasn't the only one to do this. Beatrix Potter did it. Whenever she felt her own writing was getting slack, she turned to the Bible, finding that, by that curious osmosis art is capable of, her own writing lifted its quality. Strange that these two women on separate continents stumbled on this method.

It was the same urge that led me to the bookshelves this morning to find a poet who would lift my own work. Michael Leunig, interviewed on radio by Margaret Throsby, had just uttered a phrase that stopped me in my tracks. He was describing the sound of a Mozart sonata. "Something you hear outside a piano teacher's house." I wasn't looking for any particular poet, you understand, just somebody who had a way to touch a soul. A line or two was all I needed. It was then I found the book of interviews.

14th November, Tuesday. Canberra.

A wrecked model ship slopes in its stand above two teddy bears lying, as in the aftermath of love, on this desk. Outside a wattle bird is sucking nectar from the red bottlebrush, which is entangled with a wild pink rose. A swarm of flowers metres long. I cannot imagine anything that could better express what was the genius of this house: the lushness and loveliness of the pink roses is tangled with the erect hard crimson flowers.

Last night Jack and I went to dinner at our friend Vanessa's home. She brought out a painting by Vanessa Bell after whom she was named. She was given it by an old man who had been given it by the painter as a Christmas present. We were talking about letters and diaries as Vanessa had just been reading the letters of Vanessa Bell. She said,

"There they were, she and Duncan Bell, at the height of the war, making love to both sexes and to almost everybody, taking almost no notice of anything else, and then there were all those other women knitting socks."

Vanessa, whose husband is working abroad, is sharing her home with Claudia, whose husband is also overseas, working in Somalia on a project that seems to be useless (the old story of Africa). We had curries of various kinds and a green fresh coriander chutney I like. It's in Charmaine Solomon's Indian cookery book.

A silvery grey day. It's cool. I am making soup and answering the phone. Jack's at work and his children, Clare and Chris, are at school. After days of being useless, I think some half-cloves of garlic I swallowed whole, cured me. It is a luxury to be well.

16th November, Thursday. Canberra.

I'm boiling a tongue and making *salsa verde* to go with it. Fed up with languishing in the suburbs like a half-shot dog. I mean a dog shot, but not dead. I've been shopping. It was the green coriander chutney that inspired me but, as I was unable to find the recipe, I changed to *salsa verde*. To make it you take olive oil, lemon juice, capers, garlic, a bunch of parsley (Italian is best) salt and pepper. Chop the parsley well and give it all a good mix. You can put in chopped anchovy fillets too if you like. It goes well with all boiled meats. Some people add hard-boiled eggs, some add mashed potatoes, and change it a fair bit. The Greek sauce *Skordalia* is made with mashed potatoes, oil and garlic, serves the same purpose and is good with the same things.

Yesterday, in a thin mean wind, I came out from the periodontist cleaner and poorer by $180. Still too weak to go to *The Madness of King George*, I came home on a bus, eating olive rolls from a shop at the bus stop. Very yeasty, almost sweet, with rings of olives on top and inside them. Black wedding rings.

Comparisons of one's lot with others teaches us nothing and enfeebles the will. Many born in an environment of poverty, disease and stupidity, in an age of chaos, have put us in their debt.

This passage has been on my mind for days, as I see how riddled with envy people are. Perhaps I am too, and don't like to admit it.

The problem with the life of an artist is all around us. Some people seethe with envy when they see others enjoying success that might, given different circumstances, have been their own. There is also a thing called *Schadenfreude*, delight in other people's misfortunes.

It is a lucky or wise person who can keep quietly at work, in the dogged way that's necessary, looking barely to the right or left, envying nobody, adoring the work, rejoicing in the achievements of others, knowing they will help to make your own the greater, as indeed they do. Because no art comes out of nothing. It is all built, like a sandcastle, grain upon grain. No grain holds the castle up. No grain causes it to fall.

For this reason, living in the country is good. You are far enough away not to see the daily sycophancy that goes on. And you are not tempted to join in. You can stay simpler and more innocent, less corrupted, and get more work done. You will not be there when things are being decided, when ideas are being bruited about, when grant-givers are looking around, but so be it.

I met a critic, a sweet man, who thought I had died or had moved interstate. He asked where I had been. "Home" I said. "I've been at home." But the truth is I'm torn, I'd like to be there sometimes but I don't know where the action is.

19th November, Sunday. Braidsville.

A peacock in full cry woke me. I got up with no idea of the time. Everybody was asleep. I am in an old stone cottage, attached to the main house by a rose arbour in full bloom.

Jack, his children and I drove here yesterday. Helen, his ex-colleague, and her husband Jeremy own this sheep farm.

The caged white cockie walks up and down its perch, tossing its head like a mannequin as it turns to walk back. Then, idly looking at its claws as if at long red nails, it calls "Goodbye," or "Pascall! Pascall!" in Helen's voice when she's calling her son. There goes the peacock again, a siren in the dawn.

The dog's up. A soft rain. Small birds flit through the rain. Single magenta roses and full watermelon-pink cabbage roses droop along the arbour. Through the garden many more hang on sheds, verandahs and trees. Underneath the arbour boots crunch on a thick layer of smooth grey river pebbles.

Last night when we walked round the garden Jeremy showed me a bush wren on a wire. I love these old farms. The garden is an acre or so and extending. There are new plantings of lavender and blue salvia. Orangey-pink big oriental poppies droop among the artichokes. And all around big black pines. The house is full of modern paintings and nineteenth century portraits of Jeremy's Welsh family. Judges, doctors, sea captains, and so forth. A woman with a fan. Somebody's daughter, wife, mother. Her frock low, blonde hair swept up. Heavy gold frames.

When we arrived the children and Jack went down to the Shoalhaven river to swim at Bombay Bridge. Helen and I talked about Rosie leaving Jack while she stuffed a leg of lamb.

Later

Jeremy took us for a long walk. We crossed the river on stones and climbed the hill to a gum forest. Once there was a eucalyptus factory here, stripping branches and rendering the oil. The trees still show the marks.

There was a low dent on the land. It's called Chinaman's Drain. It was dug to take water away from the copper mines. Overgrown now, filled with soil, nonetheless after a century or so it still exists.

Bombay Bridge is named because here there once was an ex-Indian Army soldier settlement. A fireplace and floorstones, the remains of a verandah, stand on a hillside with the usual forlorn tragic air. The allotments were too small for any success.

We trudged back to the house after two hours. The gum boots were blistering my ankles. Clare was tired and hungry. She misses her mother.

The house if full of grace. Pots of geraniums at the windows. Oak furniture. It's comfortable, in that unpretentious way that comes from an insistence on luxury above appearance. As a consequence, it is beautiful.

Clare and I went off with a bag and a knife to gather mushrooms she'd seen under a copse of beech. It drizzled, she grizzled. Wouldn't put on her jacket. I lost my temper, flung down the knife like an Arab dagger and said "Go and get them yourself. I'm fed up." I stormed off, 'in every direction' as James Thurber once said. Ten minutes later I peered out of the cottage door and there she was, at the paddock gate, waiting calmly.

The country out here is lush. The roadsides are full of purple and yellow flowers.

Here's Clare with her gold heart-shaped locket round her neck. (Her girl friends give her half hearts on thin chains that neither her father nor I can do up.) She's fondling the fat orange cat. It was asleep on the cream blankets on the bed as I passed Helen and Jeremy's room when they were sleeping. A picture of marriage. Sleeping as if they had been spilt from a jug.

Before dinner last night our hosts took us down to let the newly-shorn sheep into a fresh paddock. The sheep ran out leaping as we walked down to the river. All the farmers on the river have fenced it off as a Land Care Project. Blackberries are growing on the banks. Jeremy says they're good in times of flood. A farmer nearby poisoned his and lost part of the river. How can you lose a part of a river? By having it spread out I suppose, until it's just a wide trickle.

The peacock screams like a man sighting the guillotine on which his head is to roll.

Pots of purple, blue and white petunias stand at the doors. I sniffed one. Suddenly, with the swift silent venom of a masked burglar, it clapped its velvet glove across my nose and face and stopped my breath. I peeled it off.

Elizabeth Jane Howard, once married to Kingsley Amis who has just died, was much berated by him in public writings. She says in an interview in today's paper, "I don't have any rancorous need to get my own back." She says what happened happened. She and he knew the truth and talking about it now won't change it.

There's a copy of the *Concise Encyclopedia of Gastronomy* by

André Simon here on the kitchen table. The recipe for 'Elephant Foot Stew' was too tough to read out to Jack and Jeremy. So I read them one for 'Admiral Ross's Devilled Meat.'

2 tbsp each of cold gravy, made mustard and butter
1 tbsp each of chutney, ketchup and vinegar
2 saltspoons of salt [that's about 2 pinches or $^1/_2$ tsp]
Mix all ingredients as smoothly as possible in a soup plate. Put with it the meat, or whatever you wish to devil. Stew gently until warmed through. Remove meat and grill for three minutes. Pour over gravy and serve on a hot dish and you will have a delicious devil.

This is for already cooked meat. It means, I believe, that you can grill left-over chicken or turkey or cold slices of beef.

This afternoon we are driving back to Canberra. On Tuesday I get the bus home.

23rd November, Thursday. Leura.

Home again. A wet sheet of day. Mist, rain, a dour sky, grey wet pillows of cloud. A bucket left on the back deck is full of rainwater. Pale pink foxgloves were bent laden with rain when I walked in the gate.

Like all gardeners I am forced to see my place as a stranger when I have been away. And I am consoled by some things that have flourished and sorry about others that have not. The roses are dashed, bashed by rain into spills of white wet tissue paper on the path, but the place still gives me a thrill.

Lately I have had the intellectual life of a clock. I have a choice now. Read something decent and apply myself. Or sleep and wait for sun so I can garden. I did the latter yesterday. I feel as if I've given blood. This is I think from flu and being near such inconsolable grief.

I read Peter Fuller's *Theoria* on the bus home. He is mad on Ruskin and scathing about much of the narrowness of the Sixties. At Cambridge University Fuller found himself not only intellectually isolated, but scorned. Aesthetic theory had to conform to the prevailing fashion and there was no room for Ruskin, who had dared to explore the 'beautiful' and brought his scientific interest and religious belief to bear on the subject. He says:

> Such issues hardly animated the student body in those turbulent days: neither religion nor science seemed to add anything to knowledge of the 'beautiful'; the word itself was never used without a cringing apology. Aesthetic, ethical and political issues became conflated into the same social *mélange*. Ruskin was forgotten. Any refusal to go along unconditionally with what I would now describe as the Philistinism of the 'avant-garde' was read as a sign of political conservatism, and assumed to be morally reprehensible.

When I was in Canberra last week I went to the morning session of a day-long seminar on women's writing, held at the National Library, and the atmosphere was free of ire and aggression. It was so remarkably good-humoured, so like the Seventies, we might almost have called each other 'sister'.

There were talks by Professor Bronwyn Levey, Sarah Dowse, Stephanie Dowrick and Elizabeth Weiss. A paper on women's diaries, was given by Dr Katie Holmes (a young Melbourne historian). I am now reading her book *Spaces in Her Day* about the diaries of mainly unknown women.

Speaking of diaries, Suzie tidying the book shelves found a 1976 diary left at my house by a retired school teacher, Miss Lamb. Suzie asked me where she should put it, and brought it in here.

It is a travel diary written in Italy. Overlooked, deceived, cheated, lost, feet hurting in what she calls her "beastly red shoes, with high heels," Miss Lamb travels on, hope still in the breast that's also holding the cancerous lump that is to kill her. Lonely, stalwart and courageous, she counts her change, has her *aqua minerale* and a roll, and moves on.

My otherwise Christian mother-in-law once said she believed in re-incarnation because otherwise it did not make sense that some people had such wretched lives and others had such undeservedly easy ones. If there is any re-incarnation, Miss Lamb will be one who has it easier and better next time.

The mist has rolled in. The fire smouldered and went out. I ran over to the O'Connors and took some kindling from beside their pot-bellied stove. Now the fire is burning.

Where can I get some money? There has been only one letter amongst the six bills I've had yesterday and today. I can pay none of them. But they must be paid. I am casting about to see what I can do. The amazing thing is I am not depressed. Something will happen. I ought not to have had the skylights put in perhaps. But now I have them and one's leaking. They will come soon I hope to fix it.

My frugal mother was a great spender when the cash was in. Once, when my parents bought a farm, she went to town and bought herself and me an overcoat each because "You never know how long it will be before we get another." That was the last coat my parents bought me. The next I bought myself.

From time to time Suzie walks in, peers over my shoulder to read what I'm writing and goes off. I do not know what she is thinking. At first I found it unnerving but now I think it's meant to be friendly. The bookshelves are looking like a bookshop. It took six hours and was worth every penny. Why is it some people are so gifted at order? She told me the heavy books should be at the ends to stop the shelves bending. I am advised to get a clothes line and a clothes horse. The sense of peace and order in the house is wonderfully calming and uplifting.

A letter yesterday from my friend Beverley is filled with longing for time to write:

> All I want is to go to earth and I can't. Do you ever find this happening? You must, surely?... To be working on about six things at once, all on hold for weeks, and not to be able to come to grips. The public woman has taken over the private woman.

Reading any writer it is striking, this longing for time to write. Or for sex and love say, in the case of John Cheever.

And what, I ask myself poking the fire, do I want? To write

something decent? Fame, sex, money? A bit of each of these perhaps. Love? Some of that too. Mostly I want to want nothing. Or does that only come as a ticket to death? What I really want is to write a wonderful book. One that lasts. One people love.

But at this age, almost sixty, I am surprised to say that I am happy. Well if I were not, I might not have that long to try to be. Nobody is winding their needs around my neck like a noose.

I've been offered sex but it seems too dangerous and unsettling. At one time I'd have jumped at it but now I am not prepared to risk so much for something so fleeting. I think it's possibly hormonal. The chemical messengers of the body slow down. They are no longer chariots in a race, but stately carriages. They travel the roads alright, but less impetuously. I swore I'd never be one who gave up or took a calmer way. And that if I lost the urge, I'd mourn. But I'm glad. It was so undignified, so full of pain and loss. But glorious.

I write poems after making love but, even so, it's not worth it on the whole.

Certainly at the time I think it is. But the mourning and regret, grief and sorrow rise up again and I know it was a mistake. No good saying you're sorry. It's too late. You can try to forgive yourself but you know you've been a fool.

There's still one man for whom I rip off my clothes without regret, but he's far away and that's not at all a bad thing. When he's here overnight, we go for a walk. He's cheerful, courteous and full of questions. I can't answer his questions. Struck dumb as if I've never spoken. Oh yes, I *know* the answer as a rule but it is a mixture of milk, air and water. I understand the answer as a tree *knows* it has roots. It takes several days for me to become normal again, as if there's been an elephant in the house.

I can see how people take their pleasures more and more from nature. Ruskin, drawing an aspen tree against a blue sky, wrote:

> Languidly, but not idly, I began to draw it; and as I drew, the languor passed away: the beautiful lines insisted on being traced, without weariness. More and more beautiful they became, as each

rose out of the rest, and took its place in the air. With wonder increasing every instant, I say that they 'composed' themselves, by finer lines than any known of men. At last, the tree was there, and everything that I had thought before about trees, nowhere.

This reminds me of my friend Ianesco, sitting on a folding chair at dusk near Moomba gas field, drawing a creek bed and some trees in my writing book. He was so lost and relieved of anxiety, in an instant he became a happy man. He forgot himself and became the hand that drew the tree. And one morning, as I lay in my swag watching dawn arrive carrying a tray of stars through the swinging door of night, he came over and, sitting on my swag, drew the trees while the sun warmed our backs. He drew the trees as they rose from the red silken sand. He said, when I asked how to draw a tree, "Draw it as it grows, upwards and out." As he spoke he kept drawing, intent, observing, hand and eye going like mad. He is a man affected by the cruelty of theory. Unless it was a simple drawing like this, done for a friend in her book that nobody will assess or judge, he was almost paralysed. Now he has regrouped and recovered. The hand is hobbled by the mind as surely as it if were pinned with a bandage to the shirt. He's a professor of Art.

The drought has ended. The worst drought in Australia's history has broken. It's been seven years without rain in certain places. The wet season has begun in the north with good rains. Some children have never seen rain.

24th November, Friday. Leura.

A day like forgiveness. Calm, silent, warm, not a cloud. It's easy to see why the Flood was the sign of woe and sin, and the receding of the waters signified forgiveness. The sun is glowing through the glass onto the bookshelves, so ordered, serene and encouraging.

Looking up 'devilling' in Larousse, I found that it's possible to devil fresh poultry, fish, shellfish and offal, besides meat. These can be coated with mustard, dipped in beaten egg, crumbed, then grilled and served with devilled sauce. The sauce he gives is good but complicated. In France raw foods are used, but Larousse says that in England it is a traditional way of using left-over poultry, game or meat.

Escoffier gives a recipe for devilled eggs. You fry them first, turn them, slide them out and 'besprinkle them with brown butter and a few drops of vinegar with which the omelette-pan has been rinsed.'

Arabella Boxer gives a recipe for a white devil for cooked chicken, game or lamb.

Spread the pieces of meat with French mustard and put in a small casserole.

Mix 1 tsp each of French mustard, French vinegar, anchovy sauce, castor sugar and salt, together with $1/2$ tsp of Worcester sauce and $1/2$ tsp of Harvey sauce. (This is now only sold by Fortnum and Mason so mushroom ketchup can be substituted.) Blend this mixture with 1 teacup of whipped cream, and pour over the meat. Brown the dish well in the oven, for $1/2$ hour if the meat is cold, but for only 5–10 minutes if it is still hot.

Why would you be making a devil from hot meat? You'd be serving it as it is as a rule. Funny that there are devils and fools in food. There are angels too. These half teaspoons strike me as very eccentric. I can't imagine going to the trouble of locating Harvey sauce only to use half a teaspoon in this dish. Would you be able to taste it?

Now to walk up the street and tackle the bank.

26th November, Sunday. Leura.

Currawongs are singing. The mist makes them sing. They are gargling the mist like medicine. The fire, the birds, the mist rolling up the valley like a white assassin.

I've been planting petunias. The wilted rhododendron, no better for the buckets of water I fed it before going away three weeks ago, is now dug up and in a bucket of Phostrogen. An American man passing by, seeing me bending with hose and bucket, said he didn't think water was necessary right now. I explained it is to bring the plants on to flower for Christmas. The shrub in its bucket will either raise its leaves or stay the same. It may well be dead already. The pine had taken all moisture from it. That was clear when the roots came out. One by one these six or seven-year-old shrubs have died and, if I don't cut down the neighbour's pines or move the shrubs, I'll lose the lot. They look good against the old ironstone fence so I'm sorry about this. I can either take a chance and do it now, or watch them die and move each too late as in the past.

Rose-pink hydrangeas from the nursery, each with about eight big blooms, are planted among the foxgloves now. A strand of pink pearls on the garden's white throat of mist.

Yesterday, walking down Lone Pine Avenue, I called on Joan and Tom who are up at her house for the weekend. They came to dinner and I tried to get them to talk about their work. She is writing a book, almost finished, on Julia Kristeva, he one on Chekov. Tom interviewed Judy Dench in London last year, when she was playing Madame Arkadina in *The Seagull*. He said she is tiny, very energetic and ate a bit of lettuce as a meal before going on stage. Joan said she finds Kristeva very, very intelligent, maybe a genius, but she thinks she wouldn't like her if they met. They both teach English, but weren't as keen to talk about their work as I was to hear. So chat started on the topic that intrigues and charms most of Leura: houses, their sale, purchase, renovation and who has bought what. This is not a subject I like for long. Philippa used to tell me about the bathrooms of houses she had been in once, and would never enter again, with the utmost enthusiasm. I'd stand there rigid with boredom, longing to change the subject. But she truly loved this so I could not tell her it bored me.

I get hungry for talk of what people have been thinking about. But it's a mistake to try to push people, that's clear. Hunger leads to greed. Greed to forcefulness. And that to making people feel uncomfortable. Then they avoid you and you know why.

Later

I've been to a concert: the Orpheus String Quartet. Dressed in black, they strode into the primary school hall in Katoomba. Candles burnt behind them. A potted palm on each side. They played Haydn, Mozart and Schubert quartets. At interval we drank tea and had fresh asparagus rolls and lamingtons.

Milton, a man I vaguely know, said sipping tea, "The next piece I know well. I listened to it the whole time I read a book about some nuns in a closed order." A mysterious and alluring thing to say. What nuns, what book, what order and what was his interest in them?

As I sat listening to the music it became clear that I need four big terracotta straight-sided pots for the garden. Urgently. Not much hope of buying them though unless something comes up.

Jack rang from Canberra today and said he will come for Christmas with his children. Ghilly has said she will come with John and their children for the two days before. Hugh and Cathy's baby is due before Christmas and they will come for lunch – if she's out of hospital.

And so a day has passed. The need to have accomplished something by day's end rattles me with anxiety. Sometimes it seems I have just stepped from the bath, only to be stepping back in at dusk with hardly anything to show for the day. Does it matter? Just petunias planted seems pathetic. I may have fed a few plants but possibly I've killed some with too strong a mixture. Maybe I'm depressed. John said on the phone it is catching. It was hard in Canberra watching Jack suffer. But one ought to be able to visit a friend who's upset without going to pieces yourself.

Once I remember a psychiatrist asking me, when I was his patient, what I planned to do the rest of the week before I saw him again. I said I hoped to clear out a cupboard. As I said this I saw how pathetic it was but there are times when a simple task can seem tremendous.

27th November, Monday. Leura.

A hot windy day reading *Ecclesiastes*.

Whatever wisdom may be, it is far off and most profound – who can discover it? So I turned my mind to understand, to investigate and search out wisdom and the scheme of things and to understand the stupidity of wickedness and the madness of folly.

The sober truth of the text, the heat and the struggle to get up the street like a sail in the wind, led to my sleeping for three hours.

The hydrangeas have collapsed. Wet tea-towels draped over them, anchored down with trays, are saving them. The wind is fierce and Phil said when I called in, "It's bushfire weather." But I think it's too green yet for fires.

The trees, cut down in the garden two years ago when bushfires surrounded us, have never recovered. In the fear of the fires the chainsaws went all day. Overhead the noise of helicopters combined with the ash falling from the grey polluted sky and a poisoned sun to make it hell on earth. This little chain of towns, strung along the mountain tops, is linked by a single highway. Once that was cut, we knew we were alone. The fire came from both ends of the road. Everybody was packed to flee but I could never understand where we'd go. The oval is on the edge of a valley and firestorms had come up valleys further down the mountains. Even the most experienced firefighters can be psychologically overwhelmed by firestorms. We were saved, but weather like this will always frighten us. The possibility, on a warm day, of looking up idly at the sky has been taken from us.

And now dusk, end of day. As my neighbour Bill sings, "Work for the night is coming, when man's work is done."

28th November, Tuesday. Leura.

More heat. The wind's up. Draping the wrinkled and shrunken hydrangeas with wet cloths, I turned on the sprinklers. It may be the water restrictions are still on but I risk it for once. After this much rain they will be lifted, surely.

Lily has arrived back from Adelaide with Sam. As she stepped out of the car, I almost asked her how Muttee was. I told her this later. Sam responded:

"I'm sorry to say, but she's dead."

I tried to explain that I knew it, but the question had arisen from a strong habit, because Lily had just returned from Adelaide. Sam looked unconvinced.

Lily's father has recovered, thank God. The doctor said "You are supposed to have died Richard." Well, the genes of that family are strong. Through Ypres, mustard gas, accidents and hardships of all kinds, devastating polio, paralysis, these men survived.

And here Sam is, putting a nodule in my ear to hear the small radio he is wearing on his belt.

Caro has sent me her black and white photographs of Italian markets and their owners. She took them in Melbourne and Adelaide for her food book *Fresh!*. We sat at the diningroom table, with Sam interrupting every few minutes to show his own dinosaur colouring-in.

Selling from the back of a truck, or bending over a pile of eggplant, their lavish passion for produce, their generosity, is clear in the faces of the Italian men and women she has photographed. The recipes – stuffed pigs trotters with lentils, a festival dish – she's gathered dozens I've never heard of.

Thunder now. The mail has come. A letter from Kim Mahood:

> Sally and I have been discussing a July trip out into N.E. South Australia, where Geoffrey's relatives have a property. It's around the Goyder Lagoon area, west of Innaminka. What we have in mind is to drive out, base ourselves somewhere in the area and make sorties from a fixed point. It's all very provisional at the moment, but keep it in mind if you are interested.

I am.

> We did a trip this year, 5,000 kilometres in Kim's blue truck. So I know we get on. Out to Cameron's Corner, White Cliffs opal fields, Tibooburra and other places I forget. Then to Emerald in Queensland. We parted there and I got a bus across to Rock-

hampton, and then down to Brisbane, the Gold Coast and Peri's farm. For three weeks I sat there and typed up the notes of the trip, in the tropical fruit orchard, among the peacocks and the geese.

I would go anywhere with Kim, the consummate bushwoman. Once I grew tense, when we were lost – briefly – looking, as I've said for what Paul Carter, in *The Road to Botany Bay*, says is probably a fictitious lake invented by Sir Thomas Mitchell. But Kim found it within an hour or two and by this time we were, as she said, "off the map." I asked what that meant and she replied "Frankly, this road isn't shown." Then we saw a sign and we drove into the area of Lake Salvator, yelling, laughing.

Well, enough of that tale. It's another matter and too controversial anyway. But it is salutary to go and see what historians have described, I'll say that much.

And in yesterday's mail a 1946 cutting from 'Teamwork', the staff bulletin of Elder, Smith and Co. Ltd. Somebody was going through his father's belongings and sent it to my brother because it announced our father's move from Tumby Bay to Minlaton.

THE LADIES CARRIED ON CONFIDENTLY

Our Girls Held the Fort

When the late unlamented war began, our staffs of ladies were utilised in a circumscribed manner. The girl was chiefly regarded as a medium whereby mail was typed and copies thereof neatly filed. There were a few Senior Ladies who occupied confidential and relatively important positions, and it may be guessed that these have, by the judicious placement of their mature and respected opinions, assisted occasionally in the swaying of some matters of internal policy.

There were a few, too, upon whom descended some of the less interesting and more boring routine clerical tasks, upon it being discovered that they were likely to apply more assiduity and punctiliousness in the performance than was commonly to be extracted from the youth fresh from 'The Corry'.

But in the main our Young Lady's duty began when, with pencil cocked above her notebook, she proceeded to 'take down' your 'In reply to your letter of the 14th inst.,' and it ended on the following morning when she filed the flimsy in your cabinet. You, for whom she worked, often scarcely noticed her, and many of you would have had to scratch your brains to 'place' her, had you met her arrayed in her glory en route to The Palais.

But the war changed all that. When 60 percent of you were in a uniform, and the business had to carry on or suffer severely, she stepped, smart though stockingless, into the temporary breach. Calmly and confidently, she infiltered into every clerical nook and cranny of your office. Perhaps, as a ledger-keeper, she was not always over-particular about which debit was posted to which account. Perhaps she may have been inclined to linger over morning tea rather longer than you considered essential. But we'd have been in an awful hole without her.

She has shown us that in the qualities of order and method, the ability to plug along painstakingly, to quickly master strange facts, tasks and figures, and to loyally carry out the job with a minimum of oversight, neither Big Brother, nor even Father, can show her many points.

We thank her. She has gallantly helped to hold the fort of our Security. Now it's all over, and she knows that, if the young Serviceman is to have the chance to fulfil his normal destiny, she must hand his job back to him. She's cheerfully doing that more and more as the weeks keep turning.

In any case, there's a fiancé or a 'boy-friend' in the background (or if there isn't, there soon will be), and before long they'll be off together to snare a War Service Home.

In many cases, of course, we are going to need her in the Peace Years – more of her than may be available by the time the R.A.N., the R.A.A.F. and the A.I.F. are all respectable family men, but we believe that she'll be content if once more her work is chiefly confined to what it was in the pre-war years.

I had read that women had to relinquish their jobs when the war ended so that the men could have them back, but had never really understood the impact of it.

Rain now, like the thick flicks of water a woman sprinkles from her fingers when she's dampening the ironing.

29th November, Wednesday. Leura.

The scent of lemon blossom is blowing in the slow rain. Sam went to school. The bus stopped at the gate. This is one of the pleasures of living in the country. There are a few drawbacks too. I wouldn't mind seeing a film or play without it being a day's work.

Currawongs are calling. A car drives by. Lily's on the phone to a friend. We are planning our Christmas menu. It is to be all Italian. Five adults and five children.

Later

A grim unshakeable mood. A sullen sky, tormented trees. Everything needs a heaving will to be made to work. I set to ironing, thinking not to waste the day. Things appear soiled when almost ironed. I find a stain on a trouser leg.

Did I really catch depression in Canberra? Or is it the aftermath of flu? I feel like an invalid without a disease.

Lily is speaking of driving alone across the United States. To every State to write her book. I see a maniac after her, terrifying, adamant.

Many fears are born of tiredness the *Desiderata* says. I'd like to close the day down by going to bed though it's only 3.30. And still the currawongs call and trill, impervious, eating the pasta I put on the lawn. They've pecked all day like black nerves.

I'm reading *Theoria* in the window-seat, the birds drinking above me from the blocked guttering. They flap off like black washing. Two black cockatoos scream overhead. I tell myself if there is a third my luck will change. Another doesn't come.

30th November, Thursday. Leura.

Black skies and suddenly rain. We were going swimming. I lit the fire and made soup to stiffen my resolve. I must deal with a publishing contract from which I wish to withdraw. This is no fun. Other people seem to be stronger.

A card today from Philippa at Thirroul.

This place is to me still amazingly beautiful – the beaches take my breath away and I do a good deal of walking with Nelly [her dog]. I was thinking today that I feel this is the first time I have felt a strong sort of peace and total happiness since Alexis died.

Later

We went swimming at the Katoomba pool. The sun had come out suddenly. The grim mood sloughed off. Sam sang:

> *Daisy, Daisy, give me your answer do,*
> *I'm so crazy all for the love of you.*
> *It won't be a stylish marriage,*
> *For I can't afford a carriage,*
> *But you'll look sweet*
> *Upon the seat*
>   *of a bicycle made for two.*

I said "He wants to marry her, and says he'll take her to church on a bike."

Sam looked puzzled. "But wouldn't her dress get caught in the wheels?"

December

2nd December, Saturday. Leura.

The sun's come out. Things are steaming. So's the kitchen. Sam and I are making Christmas cake, *panforte* and *torta di frutta secca*. The latter is a nut, fig and dark chocolate cake, with mixed peel, eggs and a little bit of flour. Everybody loves it. As I haven't the complete ingredients to finish any of them, they sit waiting, monuments to enthusiasm.

We went to the oval when the sun came out and played cricket for a while, continuing the game we'd left because of the storm last night. When we got home we sat in the sunroom on small chairs and watched the lightning, which frightens Sam and yet is alluring to him too.

Sam said, "I wore that stuff that goes on the tree, that sparkling stuff that droops, on my waist and on my head."

"What were you?"

"An angel."

"How many other angels were there?"

"The rest of the whole class."

"Who were Mary and Joseph and the baby Jesus?"

"Nobody."

"So why were you dressing-up as angels? To practice for the school play?"

"No, we did the school play without practice."

"What did you sing?"

"'Dashing through the snow' and 'A Christmas lullaby'."
"And what else?"
"Christmas in the Aussie way. 'Dashing through the bush in a rusty Holden ute, dodging kangaroos...'."

I got out the Christmas decorations. We tied a big gold and burgundy satin bow with fresh holly to the brass front door knob. Then began a long talk lasting several days, about whether to have the usual pine growing in its pot or a freshly-cut bigger one bought nearer the day. The cut pine is what I'd like.

Later

The potted tree's come in. The pressure from the boy was too great, so I lugged it into the wheelbarrow, up the steps and into the living room. It is now decorated. I am still toying with the idea of buying a big cut one later but wonder if two might bring bad luck.

Jack rang from Canberra, on his way to the airport to go to Jerusalem for three weeks. He's to oversee Jewish, Palestinian, Jordanian and Australian women artists, working together as part of the peace process. I asked him to bring me back pictures of the Garden of Gethsemane and the Mount of Olives. I thought about photocopying some references to them from the Bible so he'd actually know what he was looking at, but I didn't. He said he's feeling a bit sick. Those Gulf Air hostesses in their little pale blue hijabs, Hollywood versions of purdah, worry him. He might find them attractive. Well he's meant to.

I met several of these young English hostesses in Zanzibar. They'd come into the Arab hotel in their chiffon chin draperies, a blue sketch referring to the harem perhaps. Within an hour they'd be walking down the street in white shorts, the local men staring. I asked them how they withstood the stares. They said they'd given up worrying about them ages ago.

I was in a hijab after the first day, my breasts worn down from stares as stones from water. I soon found the hijab, apart from being hot in a hot climate, not all that unpleasant. I'd heard Muslim women feel powerful behind the cloth, unobserved, safe and discreet. From time to time they would greet me, in the evening on the way to dinner, saying "Oh, you look beautiful." They meant they knew I was not Muslim, but was wearing the hijab for other reasons, and that they themselves thought it a beautiful garment. Well that's what I understood from the laughter, friendliness and teasing with which they'd greet me.

Sam, keen to mend a cupboard door knob that keeps falling off, got out my tool bag. He fixed it with a hammer and a screwdriver. It pleases him to make a din. He said "I'm sorry to be making a racket." Then delighted he'd fixed it, he moved to the bathroom and said he'd take off the toilet paper holder and move it to where he could reach it. I didn't take much notice, making a lasagna to freeze for Christmas. He took off the brass fitting and is now trying to knock it back on with screws. He must have watched men working. This is not successful. I've been called in and it's obvious, banging in screws to get purchase, we can't do it.

The Christmas presents have been put in a corner to wrap. I asked Sam what his mother might like.

"I think she'd like a Barbie doll."

"Why would she want that?"

"She asked Anna if she still had hers but she'd thrown it out. She'd like a Barbie vehicle with it."

Since Lily has just written a fan letter to Helen Garner about her book *The First Stone*, this surprised me. She's thirty. Also she never cared for her dolls when she was a child. She preferred real animals. I used to pose her outside our back door, with Uncle Stan's Edwardian doll's pram, the doll's legs sticking up over the edges. Her heart wasn't in it. I took the photos nonetheless. It was her sister Caro who loved dolls.

I said I started cooking a tongue when I was staying with Jack, but actually this never happened. We lost it. It wasn't in the fridge, so we must have left it at the butcher's. Guiseppe Raniola's recipe for *lingua agrassata* was given to me by his daughter Marisa Wilkins Raniola. And this I am going to make now. It can be made with veal, when it's called *vitello agrassato*. Marisa wrote it out:

Onions – plenty sliced, about 2 kg. Olive oil. Not pickled tongue (veal or yearling). Sage (fresh) – whole small bunch. Braise all very slowly (about 1½ – 2 hours) (sauce is not brown but golden). No liquid needed, but if necessary add white wine.

Sage butter sauce is made by braising the sage leaves slowly in butter. It is important to make sure it goes golden, not brown. The onions melt into a purée. You serve pasta with these onions and the sage butter sauce. Then you serve the tongue peeled and sliced. Or if you wish you can serve it all at the same time.

There are many recipes for tongue: some with raisins and vinegar, some with a mustard sauce, an English one with a white parsley sauce, another with *salsa verde*. All are good.

Thinking about the lasagna, and wondering how well it will freeze, reminds me of a perfect meal I had in a café in Poggibonsi in Tuscany with Jack and Rosie and their son Chris. Workmen were going in to lunch there so we decided it would probably be good. I turned to Chris and said as we ate "Now you and I know why people are so fond of lasagna." The *béchamel* sauce was flavoured with nutmeg, the whole dish supreme.

It is dusk. Day is done. The joy this boy gives me.

3rd December, Sunday. Leura.

From the zigzag of one pine-edged horizon to the other, the sky arches over, azure blue. The dark green rickrack braid of the pine tops embroiders sky's blue apron. Silence. No bird sings. The roses, moved to their new bed, are stalwart. Nothing droops. They should have been moved years ago. They can have now the eight hours of sun they need to bloom well. Before they could get three to four hours at most. The nuns up the street have great roses along the chain fence and yet I have never seen anybody working there. The heavy red-black rose bends under its weight and I sniff its perfume, so much the red rose essence. It lightens my step. There may be something in aromatherapy.

In the night the set, but unlit, fire caught alight. The room was strangely warm when I walked in. Again and again it's obvious that a slow combustion heater, left with the door open and the fire unlit, could set fire to the house while the owner is asleep or out. Nearby a house burnt down while the owners were out at dinner.

Last night the Muppets film of Dickens' *A Christmas Carol* was on television. This morning I told Sam that the famous actor, Michael Caine, was Scrooge. He said "Yes, I knew he was a baddie because his teeth were yellow."

Now he has invited me to a game of cricket. "I am wearing my frog T-shirt so the flies will keep away," he says, the sack of bat and wickets on his back, hair askew. I've got an extra minute by sending him to comb it. At the oval the frogs are back in the drain on the edge. We watched the expanding rings and heard the clunks of their calls. But we couldn't see a frog. Sam wanted to drag the black umbrella through to catch one. I would like to bring one back to put into the tin baby bath below the back guttering. It catches pure rainwater and should support a frog. I remember they need some rocks to climb into the bath and some rocks inside it too. I will get all that ready today in case a stray frog comes of its own accord. They do at times they say.

The umbrella is used not only for rain but as a wicket-keeper. If the ball hits the open umbrella without a bounce, the batter is out.

Pakistan is playing Australia on the TV. Phil watches much of the day. We watch at night. I am keen to get this boy ready to play with a team. W. G. Grace's mother bowled balls to him for years, and it's said that it was this that made him one of the greatest batsmen ever. We've been down at the oval for three summers now so we shall see. Mrs Grace was possibly one of the world's greatest bowlers.

Later

A day like the dawn of the world. Such a day. Bill, now eighty, was at his gate pulling weeds as we passed with the cricket gear. "A once-a-year job," he called. His granddaughter Odile, who is six months younger than Sam, is coming to play.

Frogs calling in the oval's drain, the sun gleaming on the water, insects whirring above, Sam and I silent, peering as he points to a small brown frog. The trees utterly still around the oval, the sky so blue, a koel bird calling, and from time to time magpies singing. I think of 'the silver cord, the golden bowl'. It comes from *Ecclesiastes*:

> *Remember now thy Creator in the days of thy youth, while the evil days come not, nor the years draw nigh, when thou shalt say, I have no pleasure in them.*
>
> *While the sun, or the light, or the moon, or the stars, be not darkened...*
>
> *And the doors shall be shut in the streets, when the sound of the grinding is low, and he shall rise up at the voice of the bird, and all the daughters of music shall be brought low.*
>
> *Also when they shall be afraid of that which is high, and fears shall be in the way, and the almond tree shall flourish, and the grasshopper shall be a burden, and desire shall fail: because man goeth to his long home, and the mourners go about the streets.*
>
> *Or ever the silver cord be loosed, or the golden bowl be broken, or the pitcher be broken at the fountain, or the wheel be broken at the cistern.*
>
> *Then shall the dust return to the earth as it was: and the spirit shall return to God who gave it.*
>
> *Vanity of vanities, saith the preacher; all is vanity.*

The light pours down from the skylight. Sam waits impatiently for Odile. And I go to make ham sandwiches for lunch as we are going back to the oval.

7th December, Thursday. Mosman.

The shining sea, the gleaming sky. The Heads clasp the harbour in their arms like a pile of diamonds. The sun pours down relentless as love. I am always astonished by the abandoned, lavish beauty of this place. I am upstairs in Justin's old bedroom. In a glass vase on the chest-of-drawers, a tall white ginger flower is full of scent. Downstairs Peri battles insomnia. The night before last she had no sleep at all. After twenty-eight laps in the pool, she may have slept last night.

We went to the library and then saw that Raida's boutique had a sale on. In we went. Two hours later we came out. Armani, Jodie Boffa, and so forth, all marked down to $70 or so. It was like being a child in a field of mushrooms. You climb through the fence and run from clump to clump calling out in amazement. Peri's credit card was the knife. Only people who love to shop will understand the pleasure we had. Arm-in-arm we walked up the street and bought mince for the kofta curry I am going to make for dinner.

I got the recipe from *Fifty Great Curries* by Camilla Pagalia, which Peri brought back from India last month. I am going gradually through it, cooking them one by one. The author is a manager for the Taj Hotel Group, and asks her chefs to go into each region to discover what the village people cook. As a result recipes are being discovered which are old locally, but unknown elsewhere.

My struggle with a publisher has been going on for days. I feel it is a fight to the death. It is as though I am involved in the coils of hell. Sometimes it is quite exhilarating, sometimes the pit of my stomach drops from fear, as if filled with lead.

Today I go home. I must have a talk with Lily in line with the small corn theory. This was taught to me by Margie Taylor, a feminist doctor who came to live a while with us at Dulwich when Lily was about fourteen and her sister Caro fifteen. Margie's house held the Women's Health Centre and she needed somewhere to live while a new centre was being set up. Margie said "I operate on the small corn theory in a household." I said I didn't know what that was.

"It means that when you have a small corn and do not say so, somebody can walk past you and tread on it. You may not say anything, thinking it only a small thing but, day after day as it continues, it becomes more sore. One day the person treads on it again, once too often. You start to scream at them. They look at you, astonished and hurt, and ask why you did not tell them before, because they would have been only too happy to avoid the corn had they but known."

So we used this method of living together and it worked. In fact I can't remember ever having to tell Margie about a small corn. But possibly I did.

Anyway, come what may, I must clear up a few matters with Lily. No doubt she has found a few she ought to have out with me. It's been thirteen years since we lived together. Eventually, as Peri said, daughters take over the power and this is natural. She said "Unless a mother is involved with helping one of them, or very engaged in her own work, she is a bit of a nuisance." This seemed a dark view of the matter but true. Peri remarked that she had treated her mother in much this way and now, at sixty-five, wished she could talk to her mother at this same age. How well, she said, she now understands her mother's position then.

I saw my mother from duty in the main. It wasn't that I didn't wish to see her but it seemed a long way to Gawler. Often I felt criticised. I'd be greeted at the door and she'd see a spot on my blouse and pick at it, saying "If you give me that blouse I'll rinse it out and you can put it back on when I've ironed it. It will only take a minute." Now I find myself doing this to my own daughter. I think it must make her loathe me. I know I loathe myself afterwards.

And now to fling myself, as Lily would say, into Peri's pool. It lies on the south side of the house, salted and edged with slate, dark as an eye. There's a wall of star jasmine climbing up the house beside it, covered in white flowers. A couple of days here and my legs grow loose on their bones. What's old age but loss of mobility?

People in an aged care home were on television, waving their arms about, exercising under guidance from a stout woman as they sat in their chairs. The arms, I suppose, are the last to go. And the reason for this may be that they are continually used.

I saw two very old American sisters (in their late nineties I think) performing for a camera. They lay flat on their backs on the floor and touched the ground behind their heads with their toes. This they swore was the source of their vigour. Ever since I saw that I've been flinging my toes over my head nightly, but lately I've let it lapse. You have to keep such a thing up, or you wake up one day and find you can no longer do it. Then it takes forever to get your flexibility back.

Dear Phil said last week – before he went to hospital for his heart operation – "Oh you can run! You are so lucky to be able to run." I'd been describing a cricket game with Sam. A thing like that one takes so for granted. I feel as if I ought to go out and run round the block, either in gratitude or to make sure I am keeping it going.

After the swim I'm off to see *Smoke*, a film Peri says she loved. Then the train home.

Later

Smoke is about the human soul. It's one of those films you come out from, hardly able to wait to be kind to someone. People should stand outside with buckets asking for money. Suddenly I fell down on my knees. It seemed to me I must have slipped on oil or peel, but there was nothing there. People were startled and kind, asking if I was alright. Then in the train I saw that the heel of my shoe had worn down and exposed the slick white plastic inside.

8th December, Friday. Leura.

Peri must have an operation and says she'll lose a summer if she can't swim for months. So she's trying to have it delayed until winter. Her great theme is how many summers are left. I never saw anybody so mad about summer.

I saw Roald Dahl's *Gypsy Summer* at Peri's. He speaks of his mother, who was widowed young, in the most adoring way. She rowed all six of her children, plus a couple of others, in all weathers to an island. He said it made them all quite fearless. No life-saving devices on the row-boat, nothing but her strong arms and courage and the thrill of it.

Last Sunday Sam set off on his rollerblades to show Odile how he can skate. Lying on the sunroom bed reading, I asked casually "Do you have a mouth guard?"

"No," he said.

Not knowing much about these blades I let him go. Next moment a fearful cry. Blood everywhere. The two front teeth he lost at three, from an accident on a slippery-dip, were just being replaced with his second ones. He seldom cries, but cried for half an hour. I put a packet of frozen peas on his mouth and he lay on the couch by the Christmas tree. Odile helped me get the rollerblades off. An hour later he was unrecognisable. I was close to tears. Those new teeth. Not even properly through. When I opened his mouth I could see damage had been done. But Lily said, when she came in from the city, "Mum, you can't keep them in cottonwool."

Six days later he can eat again. For two days he could only sip through a straw on one side of his mouth. And lo! The two white top teeth have come through. His smile is normal after three years of a gap. "They feel like rocks," he said. Then last night, looking at himself in the bathroom mirror, he could see for the first time what all the fuss I'd made was about. Oh keep those teeth. Frankly I'd like a batsman's helmet on him, with wire guards. Forget the cottonwool. I want iron.

9th December, Saturday. Leura.

Gwen Harwood has died. A great poet and those who knew her loved her. The last time I saw her was at Salamanka markets in Hobart ... she was carrying a huge bunch of pink proteas. When we were guests at a festival once and stayed a few days in the country, we found a quince tree full of fruit.

Quinces
for Gwen Harwood

Peri
yesterday we stood in a bookshop
I opened a book

*there they were
quinces
pale green
luminous and furry
strange as green cats*

*so solid
they sit in the hand
heavy as the history
of quinces*

*remember the tree we saw
in the backyard at Cummins
we pulled up and stared
a laden tree
spectacular
against the galvinised iron fence*

*see
everywhere beauty arrives
unexpectedly
as that green snake
lying across our path
in the mottled bush light*

*once I bought you quinces
from the tree Gwen and I found
at McLaren Vale
she stood there
did she clap her hands
like a child with a present*

*the tree stood there
giving us green lamps
which we picked*

I took them to you
and put them on a blue plate
you shook your head
and smiled

there they sat
this curious fruit
that cut has the texture
of wet chalk
and cooked
turns not like water to wine
but fruit into blood

 I rang Peri's husband Bob to ask him to tell her because I knew she'd be affected but he'd already told her.
 I said Peri would like, I thought, *Present Tense,* Gwen's latest, last book, for Christmas. Or possibly Elizabeth Riddell's *Selected Poems* which came out this year too. I bought Dorothy Hewett's *Collected Poems* for Peri yesterday as I walked down past Megalong Books on my way from the train. No, it was the day before. You can lose days. You can lose money, you can lose houses, you can lose your way, you can lose your soul.
 I am making Michael Boddy's recipe for Huff-crust Pigeon Pie but using guinea fowl which he says is a good alternative. This is a mysterious pie for "it is a pie within a pie, one meat one fruit...it always causes a sensation when it is first opened, hot from the oven spouting steam and delicious aromas." There is a recipe for it in Michael Smith's *Fine English Cookery* (Faber).
 Tony Bilson has a recipe in today's paper for his mother's Christmas pudding and, as soon as I can lay my hands on some suet, I'm going to make it. For years I scorned any recipe using suet, but I learned a lesson when I made Michael Boddy's steak and kidney pudding. It was so sensational that, as we sat at this table, tears came to my eyes. I looked about. Everybody was eating and talking, and nobody noticed how good it was.

10th December, Sunday. Leura.

In the green heart of the garden it is quiet. A red and green parrot flies in and sits on a branch, a ruby brooch on a green blouse. Suddenly a wild storm blows in. The trees toss like dancers. The rain falls as if drawn by a child with a grey pencil. Then suddenly it ceases. I lie on the window-bed sleeping and watching. The gutterings overflow.

Later

Going outside to stand in the garden to find out how I feel, I find I feel fine. Fine in the garden and lonely in the house. The green stillness is so full of things. Above a bird flutters in the bird cherry. New growth from the base needs cutting back I see. There is a patch of earth, where unused palings have lain waiting to be burned, which is ready to be planted out or have lawn creep over it. Some plants need feeding to bring on flowers. An azalea has died. A dead pine, three years dead, needs removing. Here it is, the garden I wanted with such ardour. I used to stand at the back glass doors, looking out, plotting and seething for hours. And now I have it.

It taught me as I went along. Watching neighbours' and friends' gardens, I learnt. Much died. Things have been moved twice, three times. I was slow to understand that sun is needed for lavender, geraniums and roses. But in the end I learnt. Nature is inexorable. You learn or you fail. A self-sown clematis, dug up years ago from my lane, now twines around the tall gum and drapes over a birch.

There's a scarlet geranium I brought home from a man of whom I can't think now without a shudder. Last night another nightmare about him. I seem to be searching, to be in some room to which he is bringing a woman. I can't escape. Variations of this dream appear over the years. The woman is not someone I can hate. She is merely someone who brings me great humiliation.

When I think of the woman who is with him now, I remember how I longed to ask others, who had left him, what they knew. I never did. Something stopped me. Pride perhaps. Or I thought he might hear of it and punish me.

When I see women working in boutiques, locked-in canaries in cages with open doors, I am sorry for them. Why don't they walk out? But for years I waited at the open door before walking through and away from him. I always knew I would but it must be at the right time so that I wouldn't weaken and return.

His ranting and his rages I dealt with – over dinner tables in Chinese restaurants, and at his own – by mentally singing 'The nuns' chorus' and drawing pansies in my mind. A kind of mandala figure, the centre always going inward, if you don't lift your hand while drawing. I could smile with the greatest calm and equanimity at the end of his tirade, lift the chopsticks, the glass.

Why did I stay? I never thought I loved him. Now I wonder if I did. Was it merely sex? Perhaps. I don't know. Did I think I couldn't live without a man? I had another, but he was far away. Was it a contest between me and the other women? Perhaps. And then there was his bi-sexuality. It was hard to compete with women but impossible to compete with men. When he told me about going off with men at nude beaches, I turned to stone. He asked me what was the matter.

11th December, Monday. Leura.

Silence at dawn apart from the wolf whistles of currawongs. It sounds as it does walking past a building site.

Wolf whistles remind me of some of the dilemmas of feminism. Sometimes I think there's an anger and rigidity now that wasn't there in the early days. But perhaps I'm wrong.

In fact so much fire was in some of us, I remember climbing out of a bed one afternoon when a lecturer was in it, to sit naked by a wood fire and lecture him on feminism. This so bored him, not surprisingly, that I never heard from him again. So perhaps far from being less aggressive some of us were more so.

However, legislating on the human heart and sexuality is a form of totalitarianism. We ought to know better. In the search for a better way, people are always in danger of going back to old, worse ways. It is ridiculous to outlaw intimacy between academic staff and students. It goes against everything a university ought to represent: open-mindedness, tolerance and liberality.

Now here's a boy asking to have a tooth pulled. Sam is gasping, drawing in long breaths. "Wait a minute" he says. Then "Now I'm relaxed." I tug with a handkerchief around a lower tooth. I've got the wrong one. Feeling faint I tug at the right one. But it doesn't come out. So we've left it. He's cried a little and drunk some lemonade.

Now where was I? I am not saying that university staff ought to be allowed to exploit their position in any way. But there are plenty of mechanisms for dealing with that without going to the length of outlawing relationships.

Some of the best conversations of my life were over lunch with a lecturer with whom I was having an affair. We talked as if we were drawing lilies on the tablecloth. Neither of us wanted to win, to score points, in that way that can make discussion so daunting and depressing. I learnt a million things from him besides 19th century English history and literature. I brought him up-to-date on a few things too. The affair did me nothing but good. Broke my heart yes, but I learnt plenty.

Lying in the sun, reading the latest *Adelaide Review*, I laughed and laughed, and then read out to Lily a piece by John McGrath (the food writer) on the subject of olive oil:

> Years ago, in Australia, olive oil came in little bottles, produced by Fauldings. It was on sale at chemist shops. Putting it in your ear was the big time thing to do.

It's true. Mothers warmed the oil in a teaspoon over a flame and, testing it with a finger, poured it into a crying child's ear to stop the ache. What happened if the drum had already burst from infection I can't imagine. Well, I don't want to. Would oil enter the brain? Can you have oil on the brain?

Another article which stirred the memory was about sheds. In his book *Blokes and Sheds,* Mark Thompson says:

> That's not to say that women don't have sheds or other special places, but the link between men and sheds is a strong one... chaos is allowed to reign, asserting its creative force in wayward contrast to the suburban order all around. It's a place that permits the existence of spiders, sawdust and stinks... danger lurks... risks and thrill are everywhere... something happens when a bloke gets a shed.

Tony Litermans, in his poetry book *Shed,* says 'Sheds are where men go to cry'.

Sheds are also where children find their parents' love letters and tip them out. They read them out loud and are found, howling with laughter among their friends. A mother snatches the shoe box of letters and hurls it into the incinerator. Then regrets it. Well I did. A letter a day for over a year, the history of a nurse's life. That alone would interest me now.

The late shifts, the sister's fury, the deaths. The ones who lay asking "Nurse, why am I dying?" When you are eighteen, nothing has prepared you. And then the dying, and then immediately afterwards "Nurse, carbolise this bed please!" Before the mattress is cold, the bed's sterilised and, within hours, you are taking a tray to the next occupant, someone who does not know who has just died there, nor who before that, nor who before that. Nor that you may have actually loved the person you have just laid out.

And you're late for the ball and wish to God you didn't have to cope with the new arrival just before you were due off. Your dress is waiting spread out on your bed, a new one from the dressmaker. Your hair's crushing under your tiny white cone cap.

And tired tired tired, you are going to dance and then wrestle in a Holden with a boy who ardently desires to take off your Merry Widow bra. This puzzles you as you struggle to keep it on. I never could understand why men were so keen to remove your bra. Why not just kiss?

15th December, Friday. Newcastle.
Yesterday at 5 p.m. Cathy had a daughter, Sophia Rose. My first granddaughter. The baby was curled, like a bud in glass, in her crib. I picked her up when her mother said I might. She was asleep. One bare arm was out of the blanket. I held her, this new history. Her life like a scroll ahead of her, she was pausing as if gathering strength for the reading. Sam held her a moment and then Lily did. She was put back into the glass crib and slept on.

Cathy was smiling like a victor. She looked happy, amazed and as if she had come back from somewhere. Perhaps a long bushwalk. Birth, I'll never get over it. Walking in the street I looked at the people and thought 'How many births! And all these women have gone through this journey.' It's like knitting under water with life the prize.

Sam and I came here on the train after leaving St Margaret's Hospital in Darlinghurst. We are staying a few days with John and Ghilly and their two girls, Stephanie and Donna.

Diane, the nanny, is making savouries for a party tonight. Sam is talking to her in the kitchen. The only nanny he's seen is Fran on television. The Christmas tree touches the ceiling and is covered in purple, gold and red balls. At dusk the lights are turned on. It's warm and every now and then thunder sounds. Heavy rain fell while the children were in the pool. Stephanie ran and got a rubber boat and put it over their heads. I stood at the window and laughed. There's a lavishness and luxury here that is dazzling. It makes me feel as if I've come from a desert to a palace.

Ghilly's got to go to town to sing in *Messiah*. She's rehearsing *A Midsummer Night's Dream* which opens in January. Once, when we were at university, she was a fairy in an opera. Denis Olsen told her to lie down and she lay on her back looking up at the ceiling. He said, "Ghilly, that's not how a fairy lies down." She couldn't help looking sexy.

18th December, Monday. Newcastle.

A hot north wind rolls in. John's at work. Ghilly's taken her girls to see a rehearsal. Sam and I went to buy Christmas tree decorations because I'm keen to improve our tree at home. A line of parents stood waiting with their children to have a photo taken with Santa. Sam came home with a wooden signpost that says 'Santa please stop here.'

John has been out and bought a string of lights for my tree at home. He did this on hearing I had none.

There's a difficulty when friends are richer than yourself. I know it because I feel guilty. I don't envy them, but then one never knows. The heart is so sly. I am feeling as if I am taking advantage of my friends. The contrast between the affluence and luxury of this house and my own is tremendous.

It's not only here that I have this problem of being less wealthy than my friends. It happens at Peri's too. No matter how generous they are, and nobody could be more generous, I still feel vaguely guilty. But we've weathered this over twelve years or so and I suppose we will go on.

Later

Ghilly's home. We all got into the pool. Jeremy, a small blonde boy who went to town with her, dived in. As we swam around, I asked him if he sang in the opera too. He said he did.

"What do you sing?"

"I sing almost all the songs."

"Would you sing one of them for Sam and me?"

"I can't just now because I'm puffed."

So he stood still, waited, then drew a breath and began Benjamin Britten's 'When Jack meets with Jill':

"And all will be well... and all will be well..."

He stood, the water round his shoulders, singing in his pure soprano voice. Then when he'd ended, shaking his page-boy hair he said,

"Actually I don't like singing opera. I'm a Country and Western singer."

"Really! Do you sing 'Divorce' like Tammy Winett?"

"Well really I like to yodel."

And he began. We stood there astounded. Ghilly asked him how exactly it is done. He said that you have to have a break in your voice. She began yodelling, sounding like Brunhilde trying to bring in the cows. I told her to stop or it would hurt her voice, but she said it wouldn't and anyhow she is going to have to yodel in the Sydney Opera Company's New Year concert. She has some long blonde plaits in a cupboard and will get them out. We were laughing when Jeremy swam off.

The small boy, water dripping from his hair, standing there singing so softly and perfectly, was something to remember. A gift. Sudden as rain, very sweet. It was his complete lack of shyness or boastfulness. He sang naturally, as others might chop wood.

"And all will be well... and all will be well..."

19th December, Tuesday. Newcastle.

Gardenias are blooming everywhere and the scent is strong. This, along with petunias, is the smell that reminds me most of an Australian summer.

Good champagne produces no hangover. Last night neighbours came for a party. Jeremy's parents and two older sisters came too. Christopher, the father, opened the grand piano and began to play Bach. Then he played carols. Miriam, who is eighteen in January, stood beside him and sang. I wondered whether Miriam would ever know how extraordinary and wonderful it was to be able to stand and sing to her father's playing.

I remarked on this and somebody said "Oh yes it is wonderful that the whole family sings."

That wasn't what I 'd meant. It is so rare for a daughter to be able to say "I used to dance with my father" or "I used to sing with my father." Nothing can come close to the feeling of rhapsody for a girl to do something like this with her father. I don't know what sons feel. I don't know what fathers feel. But by heaven I know what a daughter feels.

The tree touching the ceiling (and you can see how this tree has mesmerised me), the people at the piano, the candlelight and the tree lights, the hands on the keys, the singing, the ease of it, the utter ease of their pleasure. I sat and stared.

When everyone had left Ghilly poured some champagne and John and I went out to the lawn with her and sat and talked a while. I get very analytical after a few drinks. Next day I start to worry that I've been a bit pompous or self-righteous. That comes with the drink too, I know.

Ghilly's in bed with a sore throat. Sam and I are going to catch the train home to Leura. I had been looking forward to the drive to Sydney with Ghilly. Five hours in a train with a child are too many.

21st December, Thursday. Leura.

From the Garden of Gethsemane and the Mount of Olives, Jack brought me back two olive boughs. At Sydney airport he had a strike of conscience and declared them. They were confiscated. He remembered, he said, a time when I didn't declare acorns picked up in an absent-minded way in the Tuileries gardens. Arrested at Sydney airport, I spent a miserable half an hour shaking acorns out of nighties, underwear and shoes, in front of officers who had no sense of humour and seemed to be vaguely terrified. There had been some drug scare or warning so the whole flight was taken apart.

The man who'd come to meet me was about to give up when he saw me, escorted by two officers, coming towards him. He said, and this surprised me as it hurt, "What have you done this time?" I explained it would take a little longer. Just how long wasn't clear. In an ugly remorseless room, I sat explaining this foolish thing. Having signed every page of the document they wrote from my dictation, I left.

Three months later, in court, the judge quoted something from

Oliver Goldsmith that I didn't understand and dismissed the case. I apologised to various police officers as I left. They were not happy. A woman from the Philippines was fined for bringing in sweet potatoes. An Italian man was fined for bringing in five kilos of beans to plant. I paid costs and told the tale.

Jack rang from the airport. I have no olive branches but I thanked him for the thought. He is bringing his two children for Christmas. Counting the baby Sophia, there will be six children. I am saying her name often to get used to it and fix her in my mind. She could float off like a feather. It seems hardly possible she is here. A person so new is astonishing, unbelievable. She's hardly yet had enough air room made for her by us all moving over a little. While she's only the size of about two hands clasped, she's had a cataclysmic effect on her parents.

Sam's counting the days until Christmas. Yesterday we wrapped presents. He is almost exploding. Today parcels for Sophia came in the post. Everything wrapped in pink.

Lily is cooking dinner. A fog is sweeping through the pines after a warm day.

22nd December, Friday. Leura.

No fresh Christmas trees left at Mr Todarello's. Sam and I took an axe and a saw and went into the garden. We cut some flat low branches from a blue cypress, and one big round branch from another pine. When we'd lugged them in, we put them in a bucket of soil with rocks and water. It fell over; enormous mess. We did it again and it stayed up. Then we put up the lights John had given us, and the new decorations.

Lily and I went to Mr Todarello's with Sam. They had a Santa ringing a bell and giving out balloons, who took that curious, sly pleasure people do wearing masks and disguises. They come up too close and, looking into your alarmed, embarrassed face, act with that mockery that hints at contempt. It is really only a game but I hate it and shrink away although I try to be bold. They sense and expect the cringe, the bewilderment.

Elizabeth, Lily's friend, is arriving tonight, and so are Jack and his children, and John and Ghilly and theirs. Although John and Ghilly are staying at a motel, they will be having meals with us until Christmas Eve. So we are now cooking.

Later

We set up a table for the children in the back room. Chris, who is thirteen, rigged up a model flying fox. He put some plastic men on it and let them slide down to a dish of custard. Sometimes they hit the custard. Donna, who is four, sat on the couch screaming with laughter. Every now and then the cries would rise up as at a goal at football. They played this game for hours. Far from boring them, repetition soothes and delights them. They can go to sleep with the game they were playing between their beds, and get up and begin again, and play it all day, and all the next day too.

Virginia Pak-Poy and Lily as children used to play cards like this. Then they'd begin a touch-chase game and do that for days. Barbara Pak-Poy used to say, because of her three black-haired daughters, that when Lily was there it was as though a silk-worm had used the brush.

Elizabeth brought mussels and prawns from Bondi and Lily made spaghetti marinara.

24th December, Sunday. Leura.

This morning we walked round to see Cheryl Maddocks' garden because it is going to be in the Open Garden Scheme next year and she'd invited me to bring John and Ghilly. It is blowsy after spring, full of pink roses, silver leaves, white flowers, bits of purple and blue, and splashes of yellow. It's a certain look. Like a woman rising dishevelled from bed. John took some photographs of us as we walked around, the gravel crunching underfoot, bees buzzing and a currawong calling.

John and Ghilly had to leave today because their daughter Stephanie wants to be at home for Christmas morning. So we opened our presents from each other.

Later

Lily brought in candles and put on dance music. I sat and watched everybody dance.

25th December, Monday. Leura.

The children and I went to church. Jack and Lily slept in. It was very cold. I sat them under the window with the green dragon with purple wings Sam likes. We got there ten minutes early because I thought it would be packed. But it was only half full. This is St Albans, the one which burnt down. It's Anglican. St Bonadventure's, the Catholic one, is no doubt crammed and overflowing with people standing in the aisles and at the back. I've been to St Albans in other years when it has been crowded, that is why we went early.

"Once in royal David's city stood a lowly cattle shed..."

Sam understands this because he wanted a donkey and a shed for our nativity scene. He got a box and stood them all in it when we first set it up. I said I'd try to find a donkey as it's made a big impression on him.

We began to walk back shivering but Jack drove up to take us home.

Sam had come into my room before six, ready to open his stocking. He went and got it from the fireplace. I asked if the reindeers' carrots had been eaten and the biscuits and milk. We opened the stocking. A waterproof watch fell out. He has been fixated on watches for a year or so, yet he can't quite tell the time. Then some books, shorts, and so forth. The cold chill of disappointment came over him. "I thought it would have more big lumps poking out," he said.

So I took him into the living room and showed him the bike his mother had renovated and painted, standing wrapped beside the tree. Chris stumbled out and helped him tear off the paper. The bike seemed to intimidate Sam. He sat there in his tartan pyjamas shivering. So, keen to keep a good memory for him of this, probably his last year of believing in Santa, I suggested he open his present from Lily's friend Elizabeth. He was so nervous and shaken he asked Chris to open it for him as he couldn't tear off the paper.

Lily came out in her dressing gown. Realising he thought the bike was from Santa – well he'd been told so by me – she gave me a stunned look and went to the bathroom. I walked down a little later and she came out crying and saying "But Mum, that's my only present for him." So I said I'd go and explain it was from her. Sam said "I knew it wasn't from Santa because of the wrapping." Yet earlier he had said the reason for the front wheel being painted white, and the back not (Lily having run out of time), was that ash had got on it coming down the chimney.

So Lily stopped crying and got him onto the bike to test that it fitted – to see whether his feet would touch the ground on both sides while he sat on it. They did. By this time Clare and Jack had come out, so now the other stockings were opened.

By the time church was over I thought eating a lot might help keep us calm. We had a dozen eggs scrambled with fried halves of tomatoes and slices of fried ham and toast. Clare stood beside the stove and sang *Silent Night* in Japanese.

The plan was to wait for Hugh, Cathy and the baby, and Martina, one of Cathy's sisters, to arrive before we opened the rest of the presents. So the children went back to their men and custard game. I don't like people playing with food or wasting it, but in this case the custard was left-over from their dessert the day before and would have been wasted anyway. Because it was raining hard and the house so crowded, I was willing to stretch a point. In fact I'd have made them a bucket of custard if that would have kept them happy.

Hugh and Cathy brought seafood for lunch from the fish markets. While Hugh gave out the presents Cathy fed Sophia. We took turns, opening, exclaiming over and showing our presents around. Hugh shook out the baby dresses showing back and front to us, with big sweeps of his hands like a man selling carpets. "See nice embroidery here. Thank you Lily. Thanks Mum. Thank you Martina." He was so incompetent, so clumsy, bold and sweet about it, Lily was laughing doubled-over. He shook out a blue woollen rug, crusted with embroidery, pink mice, rabbits and sheep, and showing the back said "Very nice." Then, as we cried out that it was the wrong way round, he turned the other end up. He seemed unable, and we seemed incapable of telling him, to show the front. These sweet ineptitudes. So big, full of tenderness and misunderstanding.

Then we went in to lunch and the baby was laid back in her crib, not too close to the fire. As it was cold and wet we had lit the wood fire. Jack and I had made mayonnaise and we had this on the prawns with a hot potato and dill salad.

Later, ready to stuff the turkey for dinner, I was dissuaded. Nobody wanted it. I said that it's a tradition and I must cook it. If I didn't people would always remember and perhaps regret it. But in the end we carved more off the leg of ham and had more salad and then danced.

26th December, Tuesday. Leura.

A sunny day at last. The house looks as if an army had slept here and plucked chooks. Now we must go swimming.

After lunch Lily packed and went to Sydney to a party. Jack and I took the children to the Katoomba pool. People lay on the grass on towels in the sun. Mothers watched children striding up and down the baby pool, splashing and yelling.

We played cricket with the children at the oval. 'Overall' Sam still calls it, though I've spelt it and explained overalls are worn for work. When I last corrected him, he said "Yes I know. You wear overalls and we play cricket at the overall." So I've left it at that. Like the bicycle's one white tyre and one unpainted tyre, things can be the same but different.

27th December, Wednesday. Leura.

In the night it rained. Fog and mist arrive from time to time. What the difference is I have never known. Perhaps I ought to say fog or mist.

In the last four days we've used thirteen litres of milk and five dozen eggs. There have been ten loads of washing done and the drier hummed until it began to burn. I've had it. Stonkered is the expression that fits best. Not unhappy. Far from it. Just halted. After turkey soup, a tradition here and one of my favourite dishes – a sort of unfashionable boiled-up dish of bones and fresh vegetables served with plain boiled spaghetti – the last friends left. I washed up and went to sleep in the back room.

The long rows of ordered books Suzie spent six hours arranging, have been taken out to prop up train tracks, so now Raymond Carver is in India and Marcella Hazan among the poets, and I can't begin to tackle that maze. I suppose to a child a book is a book and a shelf is where they go, so putting them back seemed simple enough to them.

It's dusk. Cicadas are thrumming. A currawong, sitting on a curved bough of an apple tree, is watching a white sheet I've hung there to dry. He is watching like a hunter. If it moves he's going to kill it. What he doesn't know is that a week ago it was worn by a member of the tribe of Israel.

28th December, Thursday. Leura.

Leonardo da Vinci wrote this in his notebook:

> We have no lack of system or device to measure and to parcel out these poor days of ours; wherein it should be our pleasure that they be not squandered or suffered to pass away in vain, and without meed of honour, leaving no record of themselves in the minds of men; to the end that this our poor course may not be sped in vain.

The days so run together, they seem a river of light and dark. It's difficult to measure out the days they've become so melded in my memory. But this I do know. Last night I went to a party. We sat on the back verandah in the dusk until it got cold. Then we went in by the wood fire. We had a dinner of poached salmon trout, boned stuffed duck and salad. Then mangoes and a Stilton cheese. Later Murray, our host, asked about tea and coffee, "What is your heart's desire?" I asked for another glass of wine.

Then I asked people what was really their heart's desire. Not unnaturally some were reluctant at first to reply. But growing bolder, encouraged as they heard others speak, they at last spoke openly too.

John, sitting beside his wife Cheryl, began with "*My* heart's desire is to make love to Cheryl on this mat by the fire."

Nicholas, a painter who wears a big silver frog ring, said he would like to have a studio in Florence for a year. Christina, married to Murray, said her heart's desire is to have a broadcaster who would buy all the films she made.

Tom, pale, leaning against the lintel, said "I would like people to be able to get on together." And this was no pious wish. It was from the heart. At the university where he is a professor (he's the one who writes on Chekov) two groups of women are fighting who, in his belief, ought not to be. He admires both groups and it makes him ill to watch and be helpless, no matter how he tries, to bridge the gulf.

I said "I would like to write a book of short stories."

"Not a novel? Aren't short stories out of date? Unfashionable?"

"The short story is to me the perfect form, the inscrutable art of perfection. As if you held your hands out for a moment and cupped in them a moment of life itself. A short story leaves me shaken as if a lion roared in my ear outside my tent."

Then Murray, who had fudged with a few passages of elegant procrastination, said "Alright. If you really want to know my heart's desire, I'll tell you! I would like to make an original contribution to the legal system in this country. But now I see it's becoming more and more unlikely, as time passes, that I will."

Riches galore lie about in lives, but hearts' desires?

When I stood up to go, Murray said he would walk me home. I protested that it wasn't far and I'd walk under the pines but he said he had to walk Banjo (the dog) anyway. So we set off. Earlier Murray had crossed the room to sit beside Christina on the sofa and had wearily laid his head on her shoulder like a child.

29th December, Friday. Leura.

Sun, birds, roses. This is the wettest summer. Almost every afternoon the fog slinks up between the pines like a ladder in a stocking. One minute it's not there, the next it is. A silent white puff.

Nan gave me a lift to Katoomba to buy food. We laughed. She calls me her third daughter. She's seen a lot and thought it over. For all the flash events in her life as a judge's wife, she's never been impressed. Astute, quiet, laughing, she finds things droll.

The washing machine still whirrs on. Three loads a day, or four. I enjoy it, this cleaning. There are other things I enjoy more but there is a satisfaction to be had from cleaning that's hardly ever mentioned. The last late Christmas cards have arrived along with an invitation to go to Busselton in WA for a writers' festival in March. It's after Adelaide's Writers' Week so I can fly on from there.

Strangely soft shearers' sheets are on my bed. My sister-in-law Anne gave them to me when I left for the desert with my swag. She said "You need something soft. Here have some shearers' sheets."

I never see the moon nowadays. That's what happens when you sleep indoors. Whenever I come back from a desert trip I don't like ceilings. I sent my book off, about two-thirds done, hopefully to garner interest, and was told that people aren't interested in deserts. The reader said "At least I'm not." But I'll plug on. Some people must be.

Speaking of deserts, Jack brought back traditional Palestinian headware as gifts. Wearing a red and white checked djebelah I went over to show Nan and Phil. I forgot I had it on when I took out a rubbish bin to the path. I smiled at a man passing by and wished him "Happy Christmas." He quickened his pace and hurried silently away.

30th December, Saturday. Leura.

Reading the papers in bed I let time run. Then, because friends were coming to lunch, I had to run to the shops. Jeff, the man who helps me in the garden, mowed the lawn. With a mosquito lamp burning and lavender laid about – because of what's possibly a medieval and wrong idea that it repels mosquitos – we had lunch under the trees.

Gail lay in the hammock while Ian, her husband, rocked her. Ian taught me English when I first went to Adelaide University. He's a professor now in Perth and Gail teaches French in Sydney. They've a marriage separated by four states.

I was happy. We talked about our children, writing (he's a poet), writers and friends. The sun faded so we went inside and kept going. Luckily the wine ran out as I was feeling very hepped up. They went off to Lilianfells resort just before six. Silence fell. Exhilaration passed and again I saw how happy I am with old friends. I act like a hermit coming from a hut in the desert. Sane I hope, but eager. But will I go back to the city? No. Can I make such friends again? Unlikely.

31st December, Sunday. Leura.

Plums and roses. After all the blood and bone and Phostrogen the roses are blooming. I gathered a big bunch of *Madame Abel Chattenay*, one of *Peace* and another of *Bonica*. I laid them by chance on a magazine 'Roses for Every Garden'. They lay on the *Bonica* roses printed on the cover. This seemed an omen, significant and optimistic. Because it's New Year's Eve, and a few days ago a white screaming cockatoo made me anxious, the pink roses meeting like a game of snap were consoling.

Blood plums are my favourite. With cardamon sprinkled on them they make a good upside-down cake. There are two in the oven now. The day before yesterday I made raspberry jam from a tray of raspberries on sale at Mr Todarello's. This was a sauce on yoghurt for desert. The jug was left on the table in the garden when Gail and Ian left. Currawongs came down and drank it. The cloth was spattered as if with blood. I tried to ignore this as an omen.

When my marriage ended, claret was spilt on the front verandah. As I walked in I saw that a bottle had fallen and broken. It flowed out like blood across the tiles. An hour or so later my husband told me he was in love with somebody else. I slid down the fireplace to the floor, my feet sticking out. I'd never not been loved before. He offered to give her up but I knew I did not want a man who loved somebody else. So I said "No, don't. I'll bring her to you."

Today Lily rang from Adelaide to say that some old friends of ours are separating. They've tried hard and long. The husband said to Lily, "I think it's just worn out. If we keep on we'll end up hating each other." So they sat around with friends talking and even joking about how to divide their things.

Tennis began on television today. I found it when I flopped down having moved from the back couch to the living room. It always reminds me of my mother. She would stay up watching until four in the morning and ring me next day to ask "Did you see Edberg fight last night?" This from the woman who had to have all her four children in bed by five so she could dine with their father, spend a quiet evening embroidering or knitting and turn in by nine. She would be wrecked if this routine was disturbed, and it often was, what with children having whooping-cough, croup, nightmares or colds. When Billy had whooping-cough our Mother said "We had the light on for six weeks!"

Two years ago at Bateman's Bay New Year's Eve was wonderful, with Hugh and Sam tapdancing at midnight with Gene Kelly on TV in *Singing in the Rain*. We had dinner on the verandah of a rented beach house.

Well there's none of that tonight. Sophia Rose is at home with her parents. Hugh rang and did imitations of the baby's sounds.

Drinking, sighing, stretching, crying. Then sometimes he plays new tunes he's learnt on the guitar over the phone to me. The phone slips from his shoulder and he begins again. "Oops. Here we go..." He played his guitar at the factory's Christmas party with their band. It's a Strad covered in mother-of-pearl. Then he was Santa on a fork-lift, shouting "Ho ho ho!" He said "I thought they'd all know it was me but they looked up and yelled 'Santa!'"

January

1st January 1996, Monday. Leura.

Resolve to live avidly with some virtue.

A gold scarf lies here on a chair, a gift from Joan Kirkby who said gold brings luck to poets. Something in Emily Dickenson. I will look it up. I wore it yesterday to give a bit of a lift to work. Also wore a butcher's apron while making plum cakes. I did not expect visitors, nor were there any.

But a conversation on the phone in the evening with Jane in Adelaide.

"Happy New Year. I hope it's wonderful."

"Thanks Jane. I hope it's good for you too. Happy New Year."

"I'm reading Marguerite Duras's book, *The Lover*. How's this for an opening?" And she read:

One day, I was already old, in the entrance of a public place, a man came up to me. He introduced himself and said: 'I've known you for years. Everyone says you were beautiful when you were young, but I want to tell you I think you're more beautiful now than then. Rather than your face as a young woman, I prefer your face as it is now. Ravaged.'

"But let's talk about something else. My garden's looking good. The acanthus I've put in, to fill corners and to stop me having to keep planting annuals with my back like it is, are looking lovely now. The cosmos is out. The *Maria Callas* rose is in full bloom over the verandah. I'm having marble pieces, off-cuts from the factory, put down as a path to the shed. They'll be cool to walk on. Tim said 'It's matter mother and it will heat up.' I said 'Tim, the starting blocks at Olympia were not hot even though it was a hot day.' He said 'Mum, don't confuse me with facts'."

2nd January, Tuesday. Leura.

Peri is coming up. She rang this morning.

Speaking of sports and Olympia, as Jane was yesterday, I picked up a book this morning and read that, because of Christianity, the Olympics were abolished in 393 A.D. by the emperor Theodosius I. I see now that writing is my sport, although I can't think of sport as the Greeks did. The word for athlete came from a root meaning 'struggle', so athletes are strugglers. Pindar said an athlete is one who "delights in the toil and the cost."

Deeds of no risk are honourless whether done among men or among hollow ships.

Peri said she's reading a gripping autobiography by Anne Oakley, the author of *The Politics of Housework*. She said "It continues that tradition of women's confessional writing of risk."

"I think 'intimate' is a better word than confessional," I said.

She agreed.

4th January, Thursday. Leura.

Sodden, sodden, a sullen day. The wettest summer. A currawong sat hunched on the chimney as Peri and I walked in the gate after buying bread. *The Pleasure of Ruins,* a re-issue of Rose Macaulay's 1953 book, has combined with the weather in gothic mood. All night a big log fire burnt while from time to time I woke and worried that I'd squandered wood, that sort of thing – useless, mad, anxious and guilty. Futile thoughts and nightmares.

Meanwhile in Adelaide Jane lies in bed with her bad back, unable to get to a physio. I'm lithe enough to grumble while lugging in the wood under the dripping sky.

Marcus Aurelius is the man for the hour. He says:

Look at human things as smoke and nothing at all... An empty pageant; a stage play; flocks of sheep, herds of cattle, a tussle of spearmen; a bone flung among a pack of curs; a crumb tossed into a pond of fish; ants, loaded and labouring; mice, scared and scampering; puppets, jerking their strings – that is life. In the midst of it all you must take your stand, good-temperedly and without disdain, yet always aware that a man's worth is no greater than the worth of his ambitions.

Peri and I read him to each other in Landseers over coffee, searching for an aphorism to send in a card to one of her girls who's sad. Emperor of Rome from 161 A.D. to his death in 180, he saw the abandonment of Roman frontiers as well as famines and plagues. Penguin have published some of his sayings in one of their pocketbooks, and it was this we were reading as we'd just bought it at Megalong Books across the road.

Here's another of his observations, which reminds me of what Jack said a few days ago about Lily, "I love her goodness." Marcus Aurelius says:

[Whatever] the world may say or do, my part is to keep myself good; just as a gold piece, or an emerald, or a purple robe insists perpetually, 'whatever the world may say or do, my part is to remain an emerald and keep my colour true.'

Peri and I sat at the table eating raspberry jam on toast discussing our girls this morning. She thinks ahead far better than I do, planning things that will help perhaps, even after she is dead. There's a clarity in her way of looking at people. Charitable, forgiving, she often laughs at selfishness. It often makes me furious but she shrugs and laughs. Then I see how funny it is too.

Too wet to go out we read mainly, both wrecked from Christmas.

I haven't been able to write what happened at Christmas because I don't know how to think about it. Also I feel it's private. That's a laugh.

On Christmas night I walked into the kitchen and saw Lily

sitting on the bench top talking tensely to Jack. It seemed strange, abnormal. She'd never normally put her feet up on the bench. She said, first taking a gulp of wine, "Mum, we've got something to tell you."

They're in love.

I began to arrange things on the sink, smiling, shocked, playing for time. "That's lovely. Of course I'm happy."

In answer to their questions, I didn't know what to say because I didn't know what I thought. And now I don't know how to write about it either.

My instinct made me reassure them, they were both so anxious. But now I see that I don't like it. I thought I did, but I don't. At first, shoving down my shock, it seemed that it would be good for Lily and for Sam. They'd have security. Of course it'd be good for Jack – a young wife, a new start. His children love Lily. It could be good for everybody. But I felt queasy. As if I'd swallowed grease.

When Jack took my arm on a walk after Lily left on Boxing Day, my arm turned to wood. I'd have lopped it off if I could. I kept smiling and walking, feeling embarrassed. At home cooking and talking, I felt cold. As if a landslide had happened. And in a way I suppose it has. I see now that I trusted him with her and he betrayed the trust. He's known her since she was three when he was married to his first wife.

And now, the question is, what is it in me that let this happen? Does she love him or is she missing her father?

Having been refused by the mother, he begins on the daughter. And if I speak of the implications of this I absolutely know I'll lose Lily and Sam to him. In the first weeks of falling in love, anybody who opposes it is dealt with smartly. It only makes the couple cleave all the more to each other. And what's said is never forgotten even if it turns out to be wise.

So now I'm in a trap. If I want to keep Lily, who after years of difficulties between us has just come back to me, unguarded, lovely, laughing and open, I must hold my tongue. If I want to keep close to Sam, I have to go along with this. The only thing I can think of is to buy time by not saying anything negative. I feel like a ship trying to travel serenely over a boiling sea.

A month ago I said to Lily, "I don't know why I'm being so fussy. But every bone in my body tells me not to do it. But I think well, it wouldn't hurt me would it? But I just can't. If he didn't want me before when he was with Rosie, it's a bit insulting really that he says he does now. I said to him, 'Look, we'd have five hours of joy and five years of regret. We've got something much better than that.'

He said, 'Why are middle-aged women so terrific?'"

Later in Canberra, one morning when I was a bit toey with him, edging round him in the kitchen, he said, "You needn't be worried, that thought has been put aside," gesturing to the shelf. "You can relax."

The day after Boxing Day, I rang Jane and told her the news. She said, "I'm like Medusa – all the snakes on my head are hissing. I knew he was like this, but you wouldn't listen!"

I said, "Well, I can understand, he's lonely, he's casting about."

"Oh piffle! You're so weak. Why can't you see he's a real Iago. Always was, always will be."

I said, "I always knew that you should never ever turn your back on a man you've refused. They never forgive you and it's only a matter of time before they take revenge. But I think my real task now is to forgive him. That's what I must do. Otherwise it will do damage to me."

"Oh don't make me sick. You can't forgive an Iago, that's just rubbish. It's impossible."

I said, "Oh do speak your mind Jane, don't hold back!" And we began to scream with laughter.

8th January, Monday. Leura.

I've been to Sydney to see Ghilly in *A Midsummer Night's Dream*. The end of the dress rehearsal had yellow rose petals falling on us. Titania, asleep on a bed covered in sequins and flowers, awoke and sang as she was drawn over a real lake with Bottom the donkey, her love, asleep beside her. Nothing could seem truer to me at the moment than the idea that magic dust is thrown on lovers' eyes. And that it is this dust, this magic, that sends these sudden storms of passion. I mean nothing cynical by this. But watching Lily and Jack fall in love – so suddenly, so either mad or mystical or both – makes the idea of magic dust seem very real.

Ghilly as Titania wore a black wig and a bright pink sari. It is Baz Lurman's Indian production of the *Dream* with the orchestra on stage in a rotunda, dressed in the red bandsmen's uniform of the Raj. Afterwards in her dressing room her daughters took photos before the wig man came and removed her head-dress and hairpiece. Outside the grey sea swelled below the window as though we were on an ocean liner.

Mary, my old friend from Adelaide, and I stood at the railing talking during the intervals watching the rain on the sea. We discussed whether we thought it possible to live with a man after a long time alone. I know it's not possible in my case. She's not so sure. It was the opera that set us on this track.

Mary has a deft feeling for the absurd, and Manichean ideals. She's breathtaking the way she lives them out in her own life. She doesn't lay her self-expectations on others. Her mother once said that Mary's ideal travelling position would be lashed to the mast going to the Antarctic. Our grandmothers were friends at Angaston in the Barossa valley. Our mothers were, and now our daughters are. Lily screamed to a halt in her car when across the road in Chinatown she saw Anneke who was yelling "Darlin!"

Mary and I took a bus to Newtown where I stayed the night with her. She got take-away from a new tiny African restaurant. Seeing the menu, the multi-plaited hair and the big smile of the young cook brought back all my feelings about Africa.

Next morning Hugh came and took me to breakfast at his home. The baby lay asleep in her iron cot under the mosquito net. Hands at her mouth, curled in a white cotton rug, she lay like the pistil of a lily.

We went to the Pyrmont fish markets and bought fish for lunch.

Then Hugh and Cathy went to see the film *Babe* while I stayed with Sophia. She cried the whole time, except for fifteen minutes. Finally, as I felt sure it was because she knew I wasn't her mother, I wrapped her in Cathy's nightdress. But nothing would placate her. "What is life but a series of separations?" I said to Hugh when they got back.

Sophia thinks she *is* the breast. As a koala would wonder what had happened to the tree if the tree were removed, so the baby must wonder when the mother leaves for an hour or two. She drank and fell asleep as soon as Cathy came home. Sitting naked except for her nappy (I'd stripped her as I'd thought she might be too hot), she slept upright like a minute Buddha. Hugh took a photograph.

Last night Julia rang. She has her play, an adaptation of D. H. Lawrence's *Lady Chatterley's Lover,* opening in the garden at Vaucluse House this week. She is coming up to stay for a couple of days. Fish-head soup is simmering in memory of our old days together when I so often went to her house at Henley Beach.

It was because of Julia I went to university. She made it seem possible. We walked between the jetties at Henley Beach and Semaphore where she lived, summer after summer, talking. There were more books I wanted to read on the floor between her back and front doors than in some libraries. I was always kneeling down looking and picking them up to read. The long row of straw hats in the passage was amazing to me. I couldn't understand how anybody could have collected so many. Those from the Seychelles were the best. From each place she visited a hat was brought back.

9th January, Tuesday. Leura.

Down comes the rain. Julia and I walked in the mist at dusk yesterday with black cockatoos flying overhead. The hammock's turned into a boat hanging between the trees.

Julia at eighty makes me see that, as long as one has a passion, an art, life is exhilarating. Some people are afraid of ageing and see illness and senility as the only prospects. Geriatric hospitals make the whole idea hideous. However there are plenty of very old people living quietly satisfying lives.

Lately I am more and more interested in the phenomenon of the unhappy, vicious older woman. A sort of harpy. Several of them have come my way in the last couple of years.

It is astounding that women, who were once neither bad nor mad, have turned so savage that they seem lost to everything but their egos which drive them with a whip. This can't be all that rare since I know three.

Is it hormonal? Surely not – yet that could be a factor. Is it loss of sexual power? Is it jealousy? Or possessiveness? Or self-loathing? I wonder if it is depression. Grief, anger and then depression can have subtle and tremendous effects. Whatever the reasons, it exists.

I am all the more perplexed because I love these three women. They are not unlovable. But I can no longer be near them at all. That has become very clear. If I allow it, then I can blame nobody but myself. Why do I imagine I can still be friends with somebody who has the syndrome? I am behaving like women who want to reform men. This is madness.

It is somewhat of a feminist dilemma. To call it into the open looks like a betrayal. Yet I'd be lying if I avoided talking about it.

I am thinking it over. Odysseus' harpies were terrible. Homer knew plenty. There's the grandmother in Beverley Farmer's *The House in the Light*.

Slowly I'm becoming convinced this cruel, vicious behaviour is really often a form of grief. And why shouldn't someone rant at the loss of almost everything that matters to a woman? The loss of beauty, of sexual power. Sudden bereavement, the emptiness of what was once so full.

Unluckily a woman who is so inflamed and wild drives other people away. When it happens (and it is mostly with older people) it often leads to cries that the children have deserted them. What has happened is that the children have had to choose between sacrificing, in some cases, their marriages or even their own sanity, or simply keeping away. Health workers, hearing the cry of desertion, are often easily convinced that the children are neglectful. How could they desert such a sweet old lady?

It is a sort of colitis of the brain. I feel increasingly sure it's a form of senility. But because it is only revealed in vitriol and malevolence, and other parts of the character remain much the same, it's very hard to convince an outsider that there has been a slip of a cog or two. A loss of generosity, a new narcissism, a bloody-mindedness, have arrived. There are no alarms. Hardly anybody notices the changes, as they're often so slow in developing. Nonetheless the afflicted person ends up becoming almost unrecognizable. It's subtle and cruel to both the diseased and their victims, who are bewildered and distressed. It goes largely undiagnosed and unrecognised.

Yet the Harpies or Erinyes in Greek literature, it's important to remember, were the keepers of traditional values. And its partly this aspect in living women and men that makes them so difficult to deal with or to ignore.

It's my birthday on Monday so Lily's giving a party on Sunday evening in Sydney in my friend Mary's garden. On Monday night Nan and Phil are taking me out.

When I go to Port Willunga at the end of February for two weeks holiday, I want to start writing poems again.

11th January, Thursday. Leura.

Off to a shaky start. The day improved. Drank tea with Nan who it was plain was trying to calm me. Because the laundry is flooded (a pipe broke) Nan did my washing. This woman, arthritic and often frail, gives the impression she would leap a fence if she could help me.

Why is it some people are channels of water, flowing, calm and sustaining, the sun shining on them? And others are sluggish, disorderly and poisoned? What happened? What made the difference? Is there such a thing as innate goodness so that, no matter what has happened to someone, this quality survives? I think so. And what of the others, the poisoned?

Day is done. The laundry floor's top layer has been dug out dripping. Beneath are wooden boards which it may be possible to save if they dry out well, and then they can be polished like the rest of the house. I feel like shouting "I survived!"

13th January, Saturday. Leura.

The plop of tennis balls, the hum of the fridge, the sound of Patrick scraping his house next door. Finally summer. Hosannah!

Roses have lifted their heads, drawn to the sun by a thread of gold. I'm a bit lifted myself.

Lily is coming home with Sam to cook my sixtieth birthday dinner tonight and then we take it to Mary's. Hugh has rung asking "What would you like in your antipasto?" I said anything you'd like to put in. But he was more anxious than that. One minute – and this is a cliché but now it's the truth – you're pasting pictures into an exercise book called 'My Book', and the next, with hardly a gasp, hardly an inhalation of breath, your children are coming with their children to cook your sixtieth birthday dinner. What happened in between? I suppose I swam along like a seal thinking the sea endless.

16th January, Tuesday. Leura.

Sixty yesterday.

In Mary's garden on Sunday night, at a long table, dinner for ten. Lily cooked two big salmon and Mary made a cake with the full number of candles. I held the baby Sophia, who looked up to the stars and seemed to be amazed. When you have seen almost nothing, everything's amazing. Her eyes were like sea pools at night. As if water stared back at sky. Then she fell suddenly asleep, breathing quietly, warm like a kitten in my arms.

My children made speeches and Hugh played his guitar while Sam danced.

Today is Jack's birthday and, because we have shared a party for twenty years, I am catching a bus shortly and going to Canberra for dinner with him and Lily.

Suzie is cleaning out my filing cupboard, the linen press and wardrobe. I watch her trying to learn how her mind works. It is a way of thinking, this tidiness, I am sure.

I dreamt of a golden boat. Made of wool, skeins looped and hung along it, in the manner of a hammock. What is this boat? Is it for the journey to death with a penny for the ferryman who takes us across the river Styx? Or is it an omen of opulence, fortune and luck? Everybody wants some luck. You can't see it, you can't smell it, but people hope for it.

17th January, Wednesday. Canberra.

"What is death, but a failure of the heart?" That's what Dorothy Hewett wrote.

Every day I go out and set my little traps, to catch the day's events like tiny panting birds. And then I walk round my traps and see what it is that day has delivered. Often nothing much. But because I love the ordinary, the ordinary arrives with peacocks, sparrows, rifle birds, cockatoos and all the rest. Sparrows began a book for me once. My neighbour Bill stopped as he walked in my gate to say, "The sparrows Kate. Don't you love these little sparrows!" I was reminded that my mother said she'd come back as a sparrow. I told him this. He began to clean my gutterings, hurling down the lumps of mud and sodden leaves, spattering the path so that it looked as though a mob of cattle had passed.

Speaking of panting birds, Anne rang from the farm and said it had been 45 degrees there the day before yesterday. Birds fell from the sky and small blue wrens came in under the verandah to die.

She and my brother Tucker gave me a swag for my birthday. A swag is, with the exception of a bike, the freest thing I know. Under a tree or beside a truck or a rock, a swag lets you sleep without anxiety. It's only canvas between you and the world, but it feels like a tent. And so you sleep, roll it up and rise rested, calmed because you've lived another night, seen the stars, heard the dingoes call. A swag is simply an envelope made of canvas. Inside you are the letter, folded, writing your text as dreams.

19th January, Friday. Canberra.

Lily said of Jack, "Mum, I've known him since I was three." I called him once when Hugh had got her to climb onto our roof and she couldn't get down. He climbed up and brought her down.

It feels alien to me. As if the family had made a marriage match. Strange in our culture but common in other countries. I have not come to this position of calm without a struggle. Now I wonder if it is too lucky and too good. If, like so many things too good to be true, it will get broken. So a day at a time, walking quietly, looking at the clouds and thinking.

Each day Sam and I go to the pool at Belconnen. Sam, rising up from the water, hair streaming, parted like a white path in sand, said "I can hear a xylophone playing underwater."

I said "What a wonderful title for a story 'The xylophone at the bottom of the pool'. We could collaborate and write it."

Last year we did 'The boy who was frightened of water', an autobiographical story.

22nd January, Monday. Canberra.

Light fell on Chris's forehead as he slept this morning, as if on an altar of stone draped with the red cloth of his hair. He lay as if he'd fallen. He talked in his sleep in the night – nothing decipherable, just chewing words – then sometimes long groans when I thought he might not draw breath.

When I see young men I think sometimes of the twenty million who died on the Russian front in the Second World War. That means that almost that many women lost at least one son. The enormity of the figures can't be comprehended. It has to be reduced to the horror of one.

I look at Sam and know that combination of food, washing, love, teaching, just everything that's involved with rearing a child.

Twenty million conversations with children. The shattered women, keening, falling, drowning in grief. Not only the mothers, but the wives, sisters, friends. And the fathers, brothers, friends. Colossal. Beyond the planets. How can the earth hold so much grief? It must move off and drown the stars.

Jack is here at his kitchen bench showing Lily a map for the drive she's to do with me home to Leura today. She's making scrambled eggs. The car's being serviced. I'm so depressed I can hardly move. Hence I suppose the talk of grief. Pull yourself together. This is not something to advertise in a family. I'd like to sleep for three days and see nobody for a week. That might cure me.

Yesterday we went to see 'The Vision of Kings' exhibition at the National Gallery. Brahma, Vishnu and Shiva, the Hindu gods, carved or cast in bronze. A sublime seated Buddha in white stone, perfect as a whale's ovary. The last rooms were full of paintings, portraits of kings, picnic scenes, lotus gardens and a curious, mad, red picture of elephants in procession with a fire engine of all things, squirting the upstairs floor of a building. Maybe it was a water blessing, not a fire at all, in the manner in which a priest sprinkles the congregation on occasions.

The show made me happy and reminded me how I love India. I want to go back. I think I'll put a bit of curry powder on my eggs.

23rd January, Tuesday. Leura.

This is summer. Watching tennis on a white couch while outside the fog rolls past. And it's not much better in Sydney Peri says, though they've no fog.

Yesterday when Lily and I drove here, the sky went dark as a felt hat. Wisps of fog hung in the valleys like blonde hairs in a dark brush. Then higher up, nearer home, thick fog made the driving hard.

Today Lily packed the last of her things and drove back to Canberra to live with Jack. Sam will go to school with Clare (Jack and Rosie's daughter). I took a walk around the sodden oval and saw the blue and white agapanthus, the orange watsonia and the orange red hot pokers on the hillside.

Now to transplant some roses. It's the fourth move for some and if they have feelings, they'll be as sick of it as I am. Why I put roses into shaded earth beats me. The climber in shade at the gate is the exception. It survives next to the trunk of a tall pine and comes out fighting, clawing the air like a drowning cat. And the roses it gives me – puffs of pink and white, more every day.

24th January, Wednesday. Leura.

I lolled on Betty O'Connor's bed while she sat at her desk in her dark green wool dressing gown and read to me:

For yesterday is but a dream and tomorrow is only a vision. But today well lived, makes every yesterday a dream of happiness and every tomorrow a vision of hope.

Then she added "It's a Sanskrit proverb and I keep it here." She nodded at her desk.

Outside the fog swirled, trucks and buses drew up at the crossroads in the dark, just like ourselves, our lives. I am so bewildered. My life's become a fog.

"I have had to learn peace, love and acceptance," Betty said and I said "Let me write that down too." So this is the task ahead.

"Lily won't be happy until your hide's nailed to the barnyard door," Jane said on the phone this morning. "Be very careful who you talk to about this. You'll be seen as jealous."

But what's the point of shilly-shallying, denying the knot that is presented? Will I ever be able to undo the knot, or ought I to use Ockam's razor and slash straight through?

Maybe I'll simply sit here putting wood on the fire, cursing the weather, listening to the black cockatoos screaming, the white ones shrieking, in circles round the roof like harpies. Maybe I'm a harpy.

26th January, Friday. Leura.

Australia Day. I went with Bill and Betty to an ecumenical service at the Conservation Hut at Wentworth Falls at eight this sunny morning. Wind wiped the windows with long green gum leaves. Outside the blue mountains swept away across the valley. There were refugees from the Sudan, members of local churches, nuns in mufti, priests, one with a silk paisley cravat. A motley crew. Somebody played a drum that seemed made of yellow silk. Others played guitars. Behind us a cappucino machine sat steeped in the smell of coffee. At the end a young nun, who works with refugees who have just arrived in Australia, spoke of settling a young Muslim fatherless family into school at Blainey. We sang 'Advance Australia Fair'.

Reading *Tobruk to Tarakan* by John G. Glen, the story of the most decorated battalion of the Second AIF, the Second Forty-Eighth, I sat in the train weeping. I read it because Hugh was in El Alamein Company at Duntroon and the book had been sent to him by Jane's brother, Dink Adams. She wants to interview Dink about his army life for a family history she is writing, so I have it to post to her. Here is an extract from the El Alamein chapter of 1942, about the attack on Rommel's line:

> Then it came: 9.40 p.m. 23rd October. The darkness was rent by flashes from the mouths of over eight hundred guns. The night exploded as no night before has ever done. The desert burst into flame and shattering sound that shook the earth with its fury. Then came the dreadful whispering of thousands of shells rushing by overhead, the shock of explosion as they smashed into the enemy's guns, men, tanks and communications. The bombers joined in, raining their bombs on the German gunlines. The tranquil stars seemed to quake in their heaven and recede in horror at such destruction as had never before been witnessed in this land, as old as time itself...

This was the turning point of the war and led to the defeat of General Rommel. There are photographs of Private P. E. Gatwick VC and Sgt W. H. Kibby VC, who died during the battle and were awarded the Victoria Cross posthumously. No other book about the war has affected me as this book has. It is perhaps the detail of the battles, the naming of some of the Australian men. Perhaps it is knowing my boy could have been in a war. The German and Italian losses were colossal. Whatever the reason, I sat there not caring who saw how I looked.

Dink, Jane told me, was one of only forty-two left standing in his group. The chapter describing the five terrible nights of the battle ends:

> We thought ourselves few enough then. But surely the bravest among us would have shuddered if they could have known to what a weary handful we would be reduced by morning.

The men who were left had had almost no sleep for those five nights.

Enough. I am searching for a christening gown for Sophia Rose. And it's fair to say that I am able to do this because my own father was spared that war. I asked my sister-in-law Anne about it on the phone this morning. She said "Yes, I've got it. But its sleeves were cut because Billy was such a fat baby. It's pretty thin. She may need a petticoat. My boys were christened in it. And your mother. I'll send it certified."

Bill is my middle brother, now in his fifties, who took me across the Simpson Desert, 1,100 red sand dunes, on a nine-day camp. The desert bloomed, not with guns but as the floor of heaven with a million acres of wild flowers. People looked as if they beheld a calamity. The beauty was great, enormous. It shook us in our boots and made us humble.

February

1st February, Thursday. Leura.

It was hot yesterday when I came home from Newcastle. John and Ghilly gave a party for Jack's and my birthdays in their garden on Saturday night. They had a long table with candles in glass covers and cooked a goose.

Two days after the birthday party, John said mildly as he stood at the stove in the morning, "Jack's been telling lies about you Kate."

I ignored this, and it seems incredible to me now that I did. I simply thought he'd misunderstood something so I let it pass. Then, that night I thought I'd clear the matter up so I asked him what Jack had said. He shifted about for a while, not wanting to spell it out.

Then he said, "He says you tried to go to bed with him and he refused and that's why you are so withdrawn now."

I smiled and said, "He would not say that."

"Well he has."

Ghilly said "You know he's been saying these things about you for some time to us. John and I didn't say anything to you because we thought he'd snap out of it. We only spoke to you when it became unendurable."

It wasn't until almost dawn next morning that I finally accepted it. Like a shying horse taking the bit. And bitter it was.

Later

Jane rang today and among other things said that a book had fallen open at a page on Bologna cathedral. "See, it's a sign. You and I will be there before the year is out even it we have to sell vital organs."

Since January was hard, this may be a good omen. I cried for two days on and off. But now I've stopped, shaken myself like a dog and decided, on Hugh's advice, to put it behind me. He said "Mum, if you say anything it only winds things up. It just increases the stakes. It's like Yugoslavia." I knew he was right. Looking at my neighbours, whose ability to forgive is nothing less than tremendous, I am hoping for serenity and forgiveness. Now this may sound all very highminded, but while perfidy and treachery are always with us, so is the ability to overcome bitterness.

When one hears of a friend's treachery, it is a strange thing at first. There's a time of complete denial, a vacant space where the mind will not go. The tide is out and over the shining sand the mind – that tide, the sea – will not go. It is only some time later that the tide, the truth, slides over and the space of disbelief is covered. This is like grief itself. A calamity that the mind denies because it is too painful to be believed. In some ways it's a healing thing because it gives the mind an hour, or a day or two, to be empty, to gasp and rest. To have that gap allows a breath or two to be taken with calmness, before the truth comes in, seething with its pain.

2nd February, Friday. Leura.

Lily is missing. She's left Jack, put Sam in the car and headed for Sydney. Jack told me this on the phone last night. Since then I've been waiting to hear from her. I keep thinking of what weight of parents' anxiety there is in the world: parents in what was once Yugoslavia, in Zaire, in Rwanda; parents of street children; of the kidnapped, the missing, the sick. By comparison my anxiety is so little.

3rd February, Saturday. Leura.

No word from Lily.

Peaches and mangoes by the bucket. Mr Todarello, seeing Nan and me prowling around his trays of fruit, came over. He made us an offer on the mangoes. Then he said, gesturing to me with his head as he bent over carrying peaches, "You come back." Walking to the car with a tray of mangoes, I was thinking he must be going to tell me something unpleasant. Perhaps a cheque had bounced. I went back. He lifted up a deep tray, piled high with yellow peaches, and said "Here, for you." I asked how much and he said they were free. Nan was laughing, saying "Oh darling, what are we going to do with them?" She drove off with the last tray of mangoes on the floor by my feet and the peaches in my lap. I said I was going to make peach chutney and mango chutney and Bellinis to drink when a publisher comes tonight. It was as if we sat in a golden shower of fruit.

Sheridan Rogers' mango salsa is good, very good. When she first gave me a taste on her mother's back lawn years ago, she asked if I thought people would make it. I said, "No, not if it doesn't keep well. Why would they go to the trouble." Wrong. It is delicious and not much work at all. Here is the recipe.

4 mangoes, peeled and cut into 1 cm cubes
1 medium red onion, finely chopped
2 red chillies, seeded and finely chopped
60 ml (2 fl oz) peanut oil or safflower oil
40 ml (1 1/3 fl oz) water
20 g (2/3 oz) mint leaves
60 ml (2 fl oz) fresh lime juice
1 tsp salt,
1 tsp freshly ground pepper

Put the chopped mangoes into a bowl. Mix the onions, chillies, oil and water in a saucepan. Cover and cook on low heat until the onion is clear. Don't let it brown. Cool then add to the fruit.

Blanch the mint in boiling water for 1 minute. Cool in ice water, drain, squeeze dry and chop finely. Add to mangoes. Stir in lime juice, salt and pepper. Stand for an hour or so to macerate. Good with ham, pork, chicken, grilled meats of many kinds.

5th February, Monday. Leura.

Still no word from Lily.

Here at home planting poppies, pinks and pansies. Monica, who runs the Leura nursery, told me pansies are an all-year-round plant in the mountains. So I pulled out the old and put in the new. Dianthus, labelled as 'Persian Carpet', went in under the roses. Roses are the asthmatics of the garden. Needing fresh air, breezes and sun, they flourish when they can rise above other plants. A daily zephyr is what's needed, like a hit of oxygen and Ventolin for an asthma attack.

Jacqui, whom I walked round to see this morning, has lent me *The Myths of Greece and Rome* by H. A. Guerber. There are so many stories of characters whose names I know but not their legends. I've just read the story of Halcyone, daughter of Aeolus, king of the winds. Her husband, King Ceyx of Trachin in Thessaly, needed to consult the oracle at Delphi. On the journey a great wind sank his ship.

> Then, as the dim dawn broke over the sea a dark billow crashed over his head, and he was overwhelmed.

It sounds like grief. Zeus had commanded Iris, the rainbow messenger:

> Go, Iris, most faithful hand-maiden, to the abode of Sleep, and bid him send to Halcyone a dream telling her of the death of her lord... So Iris donned her many-hued mantle, and sought the darkling hollow, washed by the slow waters of Lethe, where Hypnos, the god of sleep had his abode.

Halcyone waited on the shore after she had dreamt of her husband's death. When the body of Ceyx was washed up she cried out and lifted up her arms to fling herself into the water. Her arms changed into wings and as she flew over the waves, trying to enfold her husband, the gods saw and changed them both into the birds now called halcyons, the blue-plumed birds which are said to nest on the sea.

Aeolus, in the heart of winter, holds back the wind over the sea for seven days after the shortest day of the year, for love of his daughter Halcyone.

Outside now, clouds wreath the houses like a spell.

Gaudiamus igitur. Making tea this morning, after talking to Marisa in Adelaide who goes to hospital tomorrow to have a breast lump investigated, I thought of Patrick Pak-Poy who had that saying engraved on a christening cup he gave Hugh. *Therefore let us rejoice.* Then Jane, also on the phone today, said she has had a two-day migraine and her back is so bad she can't come on our beach holiday. So I've asked her to cancel the house booking.

Hugh and Cathy and the baby came up for the weekend to collect the christening gown and, I think, to keep me company in this worry. Sophia and I slept in the afternoon, she in her pram and I on the couch by the fire. From time to time she'd stir. I'd wake. Then sleep would fall on us both like a sheet.

She dreams, her lids move above her moving eyes, her breathing alters, she smiles. She's dreaming somebody is smiling at her, talking to her. Then the dream drifts off like a page torn from a book. Then it begins again. Hugh and I watched her as the tide of her dreaming ebbed and flowed.

Babies are entranced looking at trees, shadows, clouds. They're lonely or bored just looking at walls.

14th February, Wednesday. Leura.

Trying for a lift, something to bring the spirits up from the cold grey day. Bach's *Partita* is being played on the harpsichord on the radio. The fire is burning and I've just had Rose's lime marmalade on sourdough bread, with tea. Nothing to complain of.

Jack rang last night. More lies. It was like listening to a curtain of bats issuing from a cave. I was glad to put the phone down.

As Betty says "When the Lord closes a door, his mother opens a window." For some reason Nan and I find this hysterically funny.

When I first heard it though I thought it a very sweet saying.

Yesterday I walked round the cliffs which roll away into the blue distance like the outstretched arm of a dying god. I've been reading Euripides and Virgil, so gods seem very natural right now. I can see Zeus up there hurling bolts.

Dusk is falling. The first stars are coming out. I read the other day that the goddess Hera's breast milk made the Milky Way.

15th February, Thursday. Leura.

Lily rang this morning. She's safe, and so is Sam who is now back at his old school.

I feel like Demeter, with Persephone rising through a field of corn. I am losing my grip. Living alone, and few love living alone more, lets the mind run too wildly. I'm hurt that Lily would stay missing for days. Jane said on the phone, when I cried and said perhaps she doesn't know how worried I've been, "She's a mother herself. She must know!"

Now I'm trying to let my house, to share it with a stranger. People have been ringing up today and I've shown some through. We shall see. One I liked – a chef. I could get lucky.

I have always felt lucky. Though sometimes I've wondered if I'm not like the mother in *The Death of Joe Egg* who keeps saying, with the sad brain-damaged child lying there before her, "Aren't we lucky? We're so lucky!" I have never had any great tragedy in my life. Being married to a man in a wheelchair made some people consider me unlucky and at times I have wondered myself. But I do not believe I am wrong. I've had a hugely lucky run.

16th February, Friday. Leura.

Let us pass over the weather as it passes over us. Suffice it to say Perth swelters in another day in the high thirties, while Leura is in the low teens. I am seething to rip off my clothes and run on a beach and on Monday, if all goes well, I shall do just that.

Yesterday people came to see the house to decide if they'd like to share it. One woman, seeing the pile of books open on the table, said "What's this! Plagiarism?" Then, answering herself, she added "No. Plagiarism is taking from one book. Taking from many is research." I let it pass, unwilling to share more than the house.

How well the ancient Greeks understood human behaviour. Reading Euripides this morning when I couldn't sleep, I was amazed to discover how real Hippolytus is, and how similar is Woody Allan's to Phaedra's predicament, though he lacks her conscience. She falls in love with her step-son, a veritable monk of a boy, and is consumed by her hopeless, terrible, virtually incestuous passion. The Greeks would have no truck with this kind of thing, and Phaedra has the devil of a time sighing and pining. It's not for nothing that Euripides is said to mark the beginning of modern psychological tragedy. He teaches forgiveness, redemption through grace and *sophia*, the loveliest form of high wisdom in that it embraces self-knowledge.

Anne, my sister-in-law, has found me a beach house at Robe, to stay at before Adelaide Writers' Week.

"You can have it for nothing because the hot water service has blown up, but there's a hot shower in the bathroom in the garage." Then she added "There's a track to the beach."

The track to the beach was what I wanted. So I fly to Adelaide on Sunday, after Sophia's baptism in Sydney.

21st February, Wednesday. Robe.

A wattlebird woke me calling "Clark! Clark!". Outside the bush is still, dark green, pale green, with tips of chartreuse and orange on the gums. Tea-trees, with their peeling beige bark, spread their trunks above the native couch grass which holds the sand beneath them. Beyond that a turquoise bay stretches away, flat, peaceful. A vista that I gaped at as I came over the sandhill onto the beach yesterday. Unbelievably lovely, the colour bright, so blue and serene, it seemed like a fabulous secret.

I flew to Adelaide on Sunday, after Sophia's baptism. Jane met the plane and drove me to her home. Her neck and back are so painful she can't yet consider coming on this holiday, though we've been looking forward to it for months.

On Monday we went to lunch at Grimaldi's. There lunching together were two men, now retired, who have had some influence on my life. One I wrote a book about. He sat, tanned, urbane, surprised, with his pasta as yet untouched before him. These moments of shock take some handling. He rose as I bent to kiss his cheek. In consequence as I was bending down he was drawing himself up. We were like escalators passing. With my knees bent I bestowed the kiss as he rose higher. Awkward and foolish I then gave the other, mercifully still sitting and not moving, a kiss too. Meanwhile Jane was chattering on about Jane Austen. We walked to a table and began to laugh, drinking champagne and Midori, a strange sweet drink new to me. But it has an effect.

It strikes me as incredible that people can meet in this manner, people who a few years ago meant so much to each other. No secret was too private, no act of love too enormous, no sorrow too deep, no grief too strong, to share. And in a restaurant now we pass almost as strangers and laugh. It's a shock but that's the way we are. But it's shameful and dishonest, though discreet. I can't admire it. Discretion rules us. And that must be the only practical way we can find to manage.

Once one of these men sent a telegram from Kalamazoo as I was packing linen to go to live with him. "Dear Kate, nervous collapse, I cannot do it. Cancel plans. I give you up. Goodbye."

Passing us as they left, the taller of the two said "See you round." He who has wept on my breast and I on his. He to whom I have written a thousand letters and he a few hundred to me. "See you round." Heigh ho girls, that's where ardour gets you.

After lunch Jane and I lay on her bed and she read aloud the first pages of the *Eumenides*. Her sweet voice went on while I fought off sleep, the wine taking effect.

Next day Jane drove me to the bus station and I came to Kingston where Anne was waiting outside the Big Crayfish

Roadhouse. A more squalid net to capture tourists could hardly exist. Buses pull in but, as I heard, "Nobody ever returns." Except, I suppose, the bus drivers. Anne drove me to Robe.

We bought fresh fish, after walking along the wharf where the boats were pulled in. One fisherman told me he'd just sold 1,000 kilos of deep-sea fish to the city market. This is the centre of the crayfish industry. Before I go, if I can find a bank, I might buy a crayfish. That is if Jane gets well enough to join me.

Anne then drove me here to the house her friends have lent me. We shared a sweet pale green melon at the table before she got to her feet saying "I must shop and get Angas from school so I'd better get going." She showed me the track to the beach, waved and walked back to the four-wheel drive.

I must work, as well as go to the beach. There's a list of African words, over a hundred, to check. The strangest thing is that I can't recognise more than two or three, although I carefully wrote each one down according to the spelling of the person giving me information at the time. Dusi, Kigwa, Kongy. What can they be? And no dictionary here will ever be of use. If reviewers only knew how hard it is going to be to check. It matters, I know.

I'm making a recipe given to me by Connie Rotolo from *Enoteca Seleno* on Norwood Parade – one of Adelaide's greatest food shops.

Connie Rotolo's Caper and Tuna Pasta Sauce

Take $1^{1}/_{2}$ tbsp best capers preserved in salt. Rinse these in warm water, if possible an hour or so before beginning the dish.

The Spanish white tuna sold as Ortiz brand in olive oil will make this good. Otherwise try Sirena brand tuna. Of course any may be used – don't not make the dish just because Ortiz isn't on the shelf.

Saute 6 or more cloves of garlic, slivered, in good olive oil with the drained capers. Chop a red chilli and add to the frying ingredients. Keep the chilli seeds out unless a very hot taste is wanted.

A cup or two of blanched cauliflower can be added at the last moment if you wish.

Take from heat and add tuna and a big handful of chopped Italian parsley. Do not cook the tuna under any circumstances as it will spoil, toughen and dry.

Toss this sauce throughout fettucini or spaghetti or spiral pasta. Serve at once with a green salad, wine and bread. Connie says you can add a tablespoon or two of cream if you wish.

Later

Thirty-seven degrees is forecast for today. As I came over the sand dune, the bay stretched out, pale blue and silver with pink clouds above. Marcus Aurelius said,

Take away thy opinion and thou wilt round a promontory and enter a waveless bay, serene and peaceful, a haven.

Dog and seagull tracks marked the sand among seaweed the sea had swept up in heaps. Rose-pink, burnt gold, cream, purple, burgundy, watermelon pink, so many shades of pink. On the dunes cream grasses were waving with low bushes of dark green wattle. And behind, the two-storey houses stared like Greek masks of tragedy out to sea. Nobody else was on the beach. I swam in the cold water sent up from an Antarctic tide.

Alone now for twenty-four hours, the only person I have spoken to is the local librarian. She bent the rules and let me borrow, although I am not a local and could not pay the $25 security deposit. I have no cash and there's no Westpac bank for fifty kilometres.

I have borrowed *Darwin, the Life of a Tormented Evolutionist* by Adrian Desmond and James Moore. Never able to accept the theory of evolution, though every intelligent, unbiased person I've discussed it with has, it's time I tried. I cannot understand how the colours in a duck's wings, feathers gleaming like a dark rainbow, could have been designed by chance. Why do we see this as ravishing and unspeakably lovely? Why do we love it so?

Once I discussed this with a Marxist. We sat on the banks of the Torrens. Then he stood and carved his intials in a birch tree. He talked of chance and I talked of awe. Obdurate and unconvinced I sat there, my red boots pointing at the water, insisting that there had to be more to it than chance because we are so moved, so overcome with awe. As I say this again now, I suspect I am going to feel pretty silly if I do find out the answer.

It's a bit like taking communion. 'The Body of Our Lord Jesus Christ. The Blood of Christ.' Almost always I find this hard to believe but remind myself that greater minds than mine have put away their scepticism, their actual distaste and repugnance, and been able to partake with faith. If Thomas à Becket and all the Saints, among millions of others, stupid or clever, naive or wise, full of faith believed, why should I cling to my doubt with such hubris? And though some of the Saints were clearly deranged, many of them were not. They simply clasped faith to their breasts and strode into destiny or heaven, flames, smoke, stones or nails notwithstanding.

23rd February, Friday. Robe.

Two children in sunbonnets were building sandcastles with buckets and spades this morning. It might have been a beach in the Twenties. A green-striped canvas awning, unique to South Australia I think, stands propped on two rods and held down at the corners by ropes and four tent pegs. Rosie takes one of these on desert trips and I have often sat under hers, working among the flies, next to a thermos and her paintings drying in the heat. I wonder if Jack has spread some great tale to her. I can't ring her up and tell her the truth. It's a mess.

Rocks emerge from the tide. Dogs run. A woman in a straw hat walks in the shallows. A fish head or two litter the seaweed. The colours are bewitching. Above this, a pale blue sky arches with a few pink streaks among soft white clouds. The sand is like powdered silk squeezing between the toes.

'I dreamt I dwelt in marble halls' is being sung by Joan Sutherland through the static on the radio. Distance makes the static. But habit makes me think I haven't tuned in properly and I want to get up to try to fix it. The other man at that lunch said he'd marry me if ever I learnt to tune a radio properly. Well I never did and he never did.

Robe is named after Major Frederick Holt Robe, Governor of South Australia, who chose the site of the town in 1846. The district supplied horses for the Indian Army and sold wool to Europe. Something went awry. Coast disease hit the cattle and sheep. Later this proved to be due to a trace element deficiency in the pasture which is now fixed by the use of small amounts in fertiliser.

Once the canning factory sold canned swan (known as Robe geese), as well as parrot (Robe snipe) and rabbit.

There is a cliff walk heading north of this street, which leads to an outlet, a sort of creek which, a notice says, drains the land for farming. I swam in it two nights ago, warm and clear, languid and salty. It seemed a miracle a drain could be so pure. It flowed under a small bridge to the cold sea.

March

2nd March, Saturday. Robe.

Today is polling day for the Federal election. All week people have been coming into the Post Office asking how they can vote as they will be at sea on their yachts. I overhear them at the counter.

There is a plinth on the lawn by the sea in memory of the thousands of Chinese who chose to come ashore here and walk the rest of the way to the Victorian goldfields rather than pay a landing tax in Victoria. Next year some of their descendants are coming from China, to land and walk the route to commemorate this journey. Peri and I came here four years ago and she stood beside the plinth for a photograph. She is one quarter Chinese.

The Darwin biography is back in the library and I am somewhat the wiser. Although I find it hard to swallow, I can now see why the duck's blue wing gleaming on the river may be beautiful but may also be the result of chance. The Duke of Argyll, always a tremendous conservative, couldn't believe Darwin either. For him it was the development of the eyes in the feathers of the peacock's tail that made him doubtful about chance. But in the end he accepted Darwin's theory and was a pallbearer at his burial in Westminster Abbey.

Each day I have swum among the darting shoals of shadowy tiny fish.

When one catches oneself idly wondering how to catch and kill a lion barehanded, it is clear isolation is having an effect.

Later today Anne is coming to collect me. I am going to spend two days with Tucker and her at Ninga Ninga Station where they live.

3rd March, Sunday. Ninga Ninga Station, Kingston.
Flocks of black cockatoos fly over screeching. It's hot. All the animals sleep in the shade. I took green scraps out to a sow about to farrow. She lay in her sty fast asleep, her long lashes pale on the dark face. Anne said "She's nervous; you know how they get when they're about to give birth." I looked at her side for signs of contractions but only her rapid breathing was pulsing her smooth circumference in and out. I would like to see the litter born. Birth is exhilarating.

This morning, as I lay on her bed, Anne talked about her life. Amongst other things that made me laugh, she said, "You know, if you don't lay out clean clothes for your man each day, well if he hasn't got clean clothes, that day is not going to be any good. How can it be? You know, it's what helped the British Empire didn't it? It was good enough for them... clean clothes daily I mean. It was that sort of discipline that helped it work."

And this she does herself. A folded pile of ironed, dark green cotton clothing is set out each day for my brother, who leaves the house dressed in this at 7.30 and returns eleven or twelve hours later.

In the living room, a sixteen-point stag head stares down. Angas, who is fifteen, showed me round the new trophies. There are six other stag heads around the room, along with various other taxidermy – fish, lizards, and so on.

Anne brought out pork for me to take to Jane when I go back to Adelaide later today. She is wrapping produce now for me. I can hear the paper rustling.

After breakfast Tucker took me out with him to look at the drain he is having dredged. I got into his ute gingerly. A gun with telescopic sights was slung on the seat, the barrel pointing to the floor. Behind us two other guns with the same sights were stuck to the rear window with flanges. Field glasses lay on the dashboard.

We drove for two hours. Plovers, tan and black and white, ran then flew away. Blue crane and duck rose from sheets of water reflecting the blue sky. Above, over a lake, a white bird fluttered like a truce.

After we'd bumped along for half an hour, Tucker opening and closing several gates (he doesn't like women to do this for him) we came to the drain which looks like a new creek. It is about five metres wide and of a very gradually increasing depth to keep the water flowing. It starts about two metres deep and is 25 kilometres long. It's purpose is to drain the water table that, as it's risen, has brought salinity to the land.

Tucker said "A kilo of salt comes yearly on every hectare from rain alone. As the country has become denuded of shade, the salt has accumulated on the surface which if you lick it, tastes as salty as the sea. Yet a third of a metre under the surface the water tastes pure." This sounded so strange I asked him again and he said it is true.

He told me that the Government had decided in 1988 to make a huge drain running through many properties. The estimated cost then was over $2,000,000. The farmers were to contribute 25% of the total cost. But then the Government decided a psychologist would be needed to counsel the farmers. Then, and quite rightly considering the times, it was decided that an archaeological report must be made to see that no Aboriginal sites of significance were disturbed. Then a botanist would be needed to ensure no rare plants would be endangered.

Tucker believes it would cost the farmers less individually if each puts the drain through his own land, co-ordinated by the Government. "So that's what I'm doing." After we'd jolted along a bit further he added,

"The Department came out and asked me to stop. Then when I got home there was a fax from them asking me to stop. Then they rang up and asked me to stop."

"Are you going to stop?"

"No I'm not."

So there it is. Now the drain stops at both sides of the public road while he waits for permission to tunnel under it. It sits with the water two metres deep. All around huge trees, poisoned by the salt, are either dead or dying. They stand grey and bare in the salty land.

When we got back to the house I said to Anne "This must be costing a lot." She raised her eyes to the ceiling and said, waving her hand in circles, "I could lap the world with what he's paying."

"I suggested to him he just goes ahead and tunnels under the road, but he said he wouldn't do that," I said.

"Don't ever suggest it. They are just waiting for him to do something like that. Then we'll be in the hands of the lawyers. And when that happens I'll not only lap the world, I'll go round the poles too and I don't like flying over ice."

Tucker used to plan to swill the salt out to sea. But now research shows it's not necessary. So he's changed his mind. It will actually save the wet lands, not destroy them.

This is the Promised Land, my mother used to say. Deer stand staring at us as we pass. Some leap over invisible fences when they see the ute. Small, lithe and beautiful, they look like a frieze on a green pot. Others, tall, haughty as camels, chew their cud and look scornful.

10th March, Sunday. Adelaide.

Writers' Week is over. It was so hot in the early part we were like dogs panting. Great plane trees shaded the four huge blue-striped tents. The river Torrens was olive and silver. Auckland and I passed like fish in a bowl after their mating, he the silver one, I the gold.

I started each day the champagne way. At 10 a.m. I'd have a glass and sit under a tree. From then on the day glimmered like the river. My heart encased in silver filigree, I'd listen to the writers.

Gwen Harwood's poems were read in a memorial. Her last

poem, about the kettle on the hob, was like a spurt of steam. She always wrote of fish boiling round her line, of light and the domestic, while thinking like a physicist of the profoundest truths.

My friend Alice and I sat in a palm's shade out the back and watched baby Kate stagger around beneath her blue sun hat. Father Ed Campion stood up to kiss me, while I pointed to the baby saying "See, we are grandmothers now." "I wish I were one too," he said laughing, before returning to the shade.

On the hottest day I took a taxi back to Jane's and at dusk we went to see the film of *Sense and Sensibility,* partly to get cool. When Marianne sees Willoughby at the ball with another woman, and goes up to him saying "For God's sake Willoughby!" it is as if he's hit her with an axe. Suddenly things fell into place for me. I saw that any hurt I had ever suffered because of a lover's superciliousness was nothing much at all. Just the way of the world. Jane said "As Auntie Maud always said 'Men are brutes!'"

I took a walk along the Torrens into the city and idly looked for a white birch tree with initials carved on its trunk by the man who had stood to greet Jane and me at lunch. It was at that picnic by a birch twenty years ago we discussed Darwin. Suddenly, moved, overwhelmed, he stood and carved his initials into a tree. And there they still were. I had been looking too low among the trees by the footbridge. Remembering he was tall I looked higher and found them.

A talk I enjoyed was given by Barry Lopez, a short story writer from the USA. He said the best thing we can hope for is to leave this place a little better than it was. You can't change the world with writing. He spoke very slowly as some Americans do. Then he read two of his stories. In one he had written "Did he kneel and crouch in the moon's light?"

I wrote it down because it was beautiful and because it reminded me of something Roger Angel, the literary editor of the *New Yorker,* once said about what he wanted to find in the fiction he published. He had once read a line of V. S. Prichett's: 'The soft owl flew over the lane.' He says,

The short adjective, instead of the expected adverb, is art itself, and makes a place and mood and time of day, an entire scene out of seven words ... This is what we're looking for in the fiction line. We want that owl.

So there it was in the tent, flying whoosh! above us, while the day moon swelled in the pale bleached sky.

I bought a book by Barry Lopez, *Grace Notes,* and queued to get it signed. It is a queer thing that when you stand in front of a magician, someone who can conjure up the owl, you find they could be anybody – a clerk, a miner, a waiter, a nurse. It doesn't show at all. Of course it's irrational to expect it to. Being gifted in this way doesn't mean they are especially beautiful or carry a sign blazoned on their forehead. I remember standing before the poet Sharon Olds and only noticing how tired she was.

A scientist gave the other talk I liked. My old friend Ianesco and I heard Tim Flannery speak on the way fishing is now being allowed to plunder Macquarie Island, because the waters of Antarctica are so rich and ours are so poor. He said it is a national tragedy and warned that other islands are to be opened up within the next few years. He pointed out that, although we may think of Antarctica as poor and barren, whales from there give birth in Sydney bays and rear their calves on the richest milk of any mammal (hundreds of litres of it), but do not eat at all for the whole time they are here. They take their calves back at six-months-old in order to start feeding again. So which is the richer place?

Paul Carter, the author of *The Road to Botany Bay,* happened to chair this session, so later I spoke to him about Lake Salvator in Carnavon Gorge in Queensland, the site of which Kim Mahood and I tracked down last year.

Ianesco had been in the larger group in which we set off on a desert trip, covering 5,000 kilometres in two weeks. It was Rosie's idea to begin with as she wanted to paint Lake Salvator. But it became clear that if we found the lake we'd get there around July 7th, the very time Mitchell and his group were there, when it was minus 7 degrees Fahrenheit and the tent sides froze at dawn. So Rosie and the others turned south to Bourke and home. But Kim and I continued north because she was going home to her mother's cattle station near Dingo and I was heading for Peri's farm. One sunny day, when we had stopped to drink tea from the thermos and were sitting in the dry grass, we made a sudden decision to go another 500 kilometres and try to find the lake.

Though now filled with grass, it certainly looked like an expanse you would call a lake when covered with water. So I'd thought Carter's suggestion, that Mitchell had been less than honest, unfair. He said he hadn't actually been to see the place himself, but that the geographer Geoffrey Finlayson, whom he'd quoted, had written in his report that it was a 'braided creek'.

"It sure looked like a lake to Kim and me," I said.

"I never said it wasn't," he replied.

Muffled and perplexed I walked away, saying to Ianesco I had got nowhere. The fact is we saw what in a hundred places in Australia is called a lake, a dry lake bed full of grass. They are not in dispute, but this one is because a geographer has declared it a 'braided creek', and an historian, in consequence, has made a suggestion which is potentially damaging to an explorer's reputation.

It is better now that I remember Ianesco's search for truth on that desert trip, the truth of the sublime. He told me that, in Kant's terms, the sublime hinges on a relation between perceptual and imaginative excess and rational containment. He photographed the desert horizons at dawn and dusk, those sublime distances which hold some longed-for truth between the thumb and forefinger of the land and sky.

12th March, Tuesday. Henley Beach.

Dolphins in a gold sea. I'm at my friend Louisa's desk, in front of the sea. Norfolk Island pines grow along the esplanade between the window and the swimmers, the gulls, the ravishing colours of water – pink streaks on the gold, with silver in between. I feel as if I've come from a cave. Living in fog and under the grey sky of days in the mountains has meant I want to live by the sea.

Louisa, dressing for work in the white bedroom behind me, is telling me a story about Tracey, a woman she met at Wilpena in the Flinders Ranges, who was her host at dinner the night before and who runs the motel there.

"She's marrying a man, a crane driver from Sydney, Tony, whom she met at the Birdsville pub. After the wedding she's going back to managing the resort in the north and he's going back to driving cranes in Sydney. She's a pilot and so is incredibly mobile.

"The wedding next week is to be in a creek bed and the local Catholic priest is quite happy to officiate, as it's only sixty kilometres from the church and anyway he says mass at Easter there for people in the camping ground. Thirty of Tony's family are coming from Queensland whom Tracey's never met.

"I asked her where the honeymoon's going to be and she said Tony had thought they'd just go to her house for the wedding night, but she didn't like the idea because of the pranks her two brothers would get up to. So she said they'd just throw swags in the back of the car and sleep under the stars for a while. Then go to a hotel somewhere in Adelaide, perhaps the Hyatt, somewhere there's a late checkout."

Tony asked her what would be the point of that. Tracey told Louisa she plans to show him, and added 'What a question to ask about your honeymoon!'

"Some men have no sense of occasion," Louisa remarks, standing up with her cup of tea and adding, as she leaves the room, "I wonder what they'll eat at the reception in the creek." She ends with "Her engagement ring has a diamond bigger than my tattoo." She's got two tiny dots of tattoos on her finger she had done when she was working in New Guinea.

I watched two dolphins rise and fall, black scissors through the sea's silk. A woman took a board and paddle and went to meet a dolphin. She drew close, raised her oar, sat watching, saw the fin, paddled fast, then rested. This went on for half an hour or so, while the dolphin led her out to sea. I wondered if she was speaking to it. At times she was only about two metres away. Did it reply with clicks and that smile dolphins have? Perhaps the smile's perpetual.

Jane came down here this morning and we walked between the jetties. A mist rose from the sea, a penumbra, and into this four elderly Greek men waded and began to swim. Out on the jetty where we walked, men were fishing, speaking Greek. Small waves passed over the surface of the water, as if a hand were flicking light, and below ribbons of pale seaweed floated over the sand. We felt we were in Greece.

Back at Louisa's house Theodorakis was playing on the radio while we had a lunch of rollmops, hot rolls and salad. Louisa lives here with Pedro who's a yachtsman and photographer. He's got a wall of books about the sea which I've been reading.

Pedro is up north on a shoot, so Louisa and I are alone. Each afternoon I sleep on an old cedar couch in front of this window, unwilling to go to my room and miss the sea. Louisa and Pedro sleep in a bedroom without a door. It opens into this room, so they can see the water all night and watch the dawn. The moon, that night nurse of the sleepless, takes Louisa's pulse every time she wakes. Dawn splashes pink around from the day's paint can. I long to live by the sea.

13th March, Wednesday. Henley Beach.

A white dot in the sea, with two smaller dots behind it, turns out to be a bald man floating on his back, feet pointing to the dark line between the sea and sky. A white ship travels that dark blue line, sailing from Port Adelaide to further up the coast. Two men are rollerblading past. Behind them a bulldog runs, its lolling rose-pink tongue hauling it forward.

Louisa has a pale green curtain, about three metres long, handpainted with the Masefield poem *Sea fever*.

I must go down to the seas again, to the lonely sea and the sky,
And all I ask is a tall ship and a star to steer her by,

And the wheel's kick and the wind's song and the white sail's shaking,
And a grey mist on the sea's face and a grey dawn breaking.

This is painted among the brown ropes and against the sky, as if you were standing on deck, the wheel in your hand, looking up reading clouds.

Marisa has rung. She had a swim with me here two days ago. She'd had a partial mastectomy a week ago, so we talked about healing and how convinced I am that the sea will help her. As we were speaking over the phone, I laughed as I could see an old stout man with a hairy back, sweetly pulling down the back of his big black shorts, bending his knees away from the tap on the path so he could run the water through to swill away the sand from his buttocks. I described this to her and she laughed and said,

"Oh! that's what we did as children, don't you remember? We were so natural then, getting rid of sand with the hose."

She then said, "I am so frightened. I keep wondering why I need my friends' love so much. I am like a child asking them to take care of me and show me their love."

I said that I thought this was a good thing. People need reassurance and love continually because we are flames burning. We must eat to live and we must have love. And it can't be last year's. We need it this week. She feels humiliated by her need – cut down, hungry for love.

14th March, Thursday. Henley Beach.

Where are the dolphins? My eyes are combing the sea. Perhaps it is too early. An old, tall, thin man, white as a gull, has begun to skip with a rope along the beach. I sit here watching the film of the sea, entranced as the arm of a swimmer rises and falls, a needle stitching the blue silk in a silver line.

My ex-husband, who lives nearby on the esplanade, said at the end of our long phone talk, "Oh! here's a dolphin going past." I said "Well send it down this way." So after twenty years a dolphin swims between us.

When I was married the wish to be included in normal society ruled a lot of what we did. Therefore we disguised the fact my husband couldn't sit up, he was propped up. But we pretended he was simply sitting there and in a thousand other ways we conspired to convince others we were acceptable. We were so successful at this that when people came into our small drycleaning and toy shop some ran in and said to the man at the counter, "Oh don't get up, I can see it. I'll get it myself." And with that they unhooked their garment from the rack, paid the man and rushed out. As a result of the struggle (and this was at a time before many young people were seen in public in wheelchairs, before science saved some from the worst effects of polio and road accidents), we were unusual in living, as we did, a very public life.

For this reason while I can be as dramatic as the next person on certain events in my life, I find it difficult to describe things that are personally shattering except in an almost dismissive manner. It is the years of training that did it.

Nursing itself has a similar effect as it causes people to be uncommonly cheerful in the face of great misadventure. The blood bottle falls onto the white quilt while the patient watches aghast. "OK, don't worry," the nurse says, swishing away the quilt and kicking the oozing bottle out of sight. "It's nothing, it often happens, I'll just set up another."

In my own case this attitude combines with another that can be equally disturbing to others, that is I am able to speak about matters that many people find hair-raisingly intimate. I was not always like this. Private and silent, I kept my deepest feelings to myself. I had to. I couldn't say how unhappy I was during the last part of my marriage. It wasn't my husbands' fault. He hadn't changed, I had. So with a dose of post partum depression I took an overdose and landed in a respirator.

When I woke up tied with rags to a bed in my old training hospital, I thought things over. I thought that ethics were for living by and it was perfectly clear my ethics had taken the breath from my body. So I decided to discard them. And without another thought and in the most complete reversal, I began to be able to talk about my feelings to several others. But my husband was excluded from this. I decided to take lovers and to have no guilt. So I took them and never, as far as I can tell, had a moment of regret. The marriage of course couldn't stand it and, already rocky, simply collapsed. And so I was free and so was he.

It is the combination of these two queer things that affects my work. On the one hand I can talk openly on certain matters and, on the other I dismiss or minimise things that cause pain.

Now I must pack to catch the plane to Perth. There's the Festival on at Busselton.

16th March, Saturday. Busselton.

We lay on the bed like plunder. Dust motes floated in a beam of light above us.

This is the man who once shot my angel. A few white feathers drifted down. But it recovered. He'd said, in another hotel bedroom, that being a poet I was like the photographer who took the picture of the starving African child sitting on the earth with a vulture waiting, watching. This picture appeared all around the world. It was on the cover of *Time* or *Newsweek*. It helped raise money to alleviate the famine but the fact is the photographer made money from it. There was criticism of this. The photographer committed suicide.

I didn't write poetry for ages. But if everybody took this to heart, there would only be art of a distant and fanciful kind. All art comes from our lives. An artist takes life and, like an acrobat, leaps and somersaults through the air. If he is right and poets (like photographers) devour others in using them for their own ends, can we only write poems about or photograph, clouds and trees? Are we never to see the human hand lifting a pot, a woman bending to the oven, staring out of a window, taking a bath? He's opposed to autobiograpical art and writing.

This is an elegant, easy-going writers' festival, started by the local librarian, Anne Mularkey. Ducks walk around the tents and dive into the olive green river Vass, named for a man who came ashore from a French ship and failed to return.

Yesterday I walked into town from this motel and came to an Anglican church. I walked around trying to get in. A side door was open and a communion service going on. Once inside I didn't like to walk out as there were only six people there. The real reason may have been that I wanted to pray.

As I walked down to the sea the words of the Cranmer Prayer Book of 1614 ran over and over in my mind.

We do not presume to come to this thy table, O Lord, trusting in our own righteousness, but in thy manifold and great mercies.

I was to give a paper on 'Writing from the edge' and it seemed to me that, for beauty and compression, nothing that has followed since has matched this.

Later

It was windy. I walked to the jetty, two kilometres long, built in a curve. On the beach is a pole with a barrel on top. It's to commemorate the barrel which once showed ships the way into the harbour. There's something about these queer local things. They're mad and human, a combination I love. There's often something both bizarre and poignant about them. A petrol drum on a rock marks the most northern point of this continent. You scramble over rocks and arrive, after days of travel, to find an empty petrol drum rusting in the spray.

Blown about by the wind, which got stronger the further I went out to sea along the jetty, I walked back to the motel.

A room like an old shed, which I'd made a bit more homely by hanging evening clothes on the curtain rods, to uncrease them. My friend, arriving in the room, said, "Kate, you know there's a wardrobe here. Why are your clothes up there?" It's often that way with us. He asks a question. The answer is plain to me but I feel so bewildered I can't answer him.

I lie there thinking 'Who stitched these stars to the sky's blue cape? You there, me over here. Below us the earth, the great plains, the sea pounding the Bight. Antarctica down there, lapsed and rich, a white light where whales browse the krill. I on this shoulder, you on the other. Dark star, we fell here from some burnt event and fate sewed us on with that old silver thread that outlasts and outlasts.' I don't say this. It would alarm him. I just stare at him. He is as outlandish and beautiful as I feel. We get up and go to dinner.

Between courses, white-faced from drink, I saw myself in the bathroom mirror. All evening I'd watched a woman woo this man, animated and energetic as a butterfly. She was as enchanting as a bird of paradise in a mating dance. He sat drinking his soup, eating his beef – nodding, pleasant, civilised and stolid. It was a salutary thing to see. I saw the way we women work for men, how we flirt and fly, dashing ourselves in their faces.

We went home in the back of somebody's car. "Accursed be the sailors that brought this madman."

Next morning a breakfast at Woonerup House, a National Trust homestead thirty kilometres away. We had not slept. A band was playing Mozart on a verandah. Trestle tables were piled with baskets of croissants, ham and magnums of champagne. I felt barbaric, as if I'd come from a desert decked out in silver bracelets to the elbows, a diamond in a nostril.

Under a big gum tree Brenda Walker was talking to her girl friend about husbands and sons. I made a few Sibylline utterances and wondered if I ought to get some emerald earrings. It was that kind of breakfast. Then he and I drove back to the tents and tried to look sensible.

Tomorrow he goes home to Melbourne.

23rd March, Saturday. Leura.

I minded Sophia Rose yesterday as soon as I got in from Perth. I fed her in a park on a bench and, although she did not actually enjoy the bottle – who would after a breast? – she took it graciously enough. Then she slept under trees at home while I watched her from a window.

I dolled her up in pink. Bootees made of knitted pink ribbons, wild things, like a pink baby chicken on each foot. A blue rug covered with pink rabbits and roses and teddybears. She was the kitchest child in Newtown and I marvelled that passers-by did not gasp at the glory of her. Instead, looking serious, they crossed with the lights, while I wheeled this rosebud around the stinking streets, blue with fumes, wondering how the world had come to be so poisoned, and yet so full of love among the noise and the chaos.

I met an elderly Salvation Army money gatherer sitting on a chair by a bank. A gothic figure with long nails and a brown curly wig under her bonnet. She proved to be one of the few interested in the child asleep in her voluptous setting, her long brown lashes curving on her moonlight skin.

We had a chat about the Blue Mountains. I found her wonderfully engaging, charming and alarming, but full of kindness. She said she's going away singing soon and wants the group to go, not to Victoria but to the mountains. There was the force of ardour in her and it is ardour I love above almost everything else.

April

4th April, Thursday. Leura.

Earlier this week I went to Canberra to give two poetry readings at Café Neruda. Before the guest poet reads, the two managers of the café read a Pablo Neruda poem in Spanish and in English. They read each line in turn, the male and the female voices alternating. It was moving. There in a suburb, while outside the cold wind blew, the sounds of both languages reverberated around the tiny café where about twenty people sat.

I stayed with Patricia Harry, a painter, furniture-maker and cook. In her garden iron chairs and benches sit under the trees. They are painted acid green or scarlet or bright yellow. Very beautiful. They are made of iron junk welded into shape by her collaborator Philip Spellman.

I sat in her study to type the new poems I read at Café Neruda on Tuesday night. Next day we went to see the Turner show at the National Gallery. I am reading Peter Ackroyd's biography of William Blake. Turner and Blake were similarly inspired. I don't know if Turner saw God but he must have felt as if he did at times, staring at the eye of the storm, painting like fury.

Blake saw God for the first time when he was only four, as his wife later reminded him:

> You know, dear, the first time you saw God was when you were four years old. And he put his head to the window and set you ascreaming.

Blake said that the Angel Gabriel visited him when he was

wondering out loud "Aye! Who can paint an angel?"

Voice: Michelangelo could.
Blake: And how do *you* know?
Voice: I *know* for I sat to him: I am the arch-angel Gabriel.
Blake: Oho! You are, are you? I must have better assurance than that of a wandering voice; you may be an evil spirit – there are such in the land.
Voice: You shall have good assurance. Can an evil spirit do this?

Blake says he then

... looked whence the voice came and was then aware of a shining shape, with bright wings, who diffused much light. As I looked, the shape dilated more and more: he waved his hands; the roof of my study opened; he ascended into heaven; he stood in the sun, and beckoning to me, moved the universe. An angel of evil could not have *done that* – it was the arch-angel Gabriel.

After seeing the Turner show, Patricia and I had lunch at Café Chaos. It is a mistake to go shopping after drinking at lunch. This morning I woke up and, drinking tea beside Patricia on her bed, said I would take back the caramel cashmere jumper I bought yesterday.

"Oh but it suits you!"

"Oh well, in that case I've changed my mind. I'll keep it. And pay for it God knows how."

We drank the almond-flavoured tea I'd bought from the baker's shop in Leura, the taste of which will remind me of this visit. It tastes like autumn.

On the train coming home, I peeled a very fresh tangelo. The smell rose like dawn. Perhaps because of the smell, I thought to offer a segment to the elderly woman sitting beside me. She was wearing a supporting orthopaedic collar and had a walking stick leaning against the seat. She declined, but this broke the silence.

At Bundanoon station, the woman asked, "Is this where Arthur Boyd gave his home?" I said it was and that the Shoalhaven River must be nearby because that is where he so often painted. I was still reading Ackroyd's biography of Blake and, as I turned a page, I saw a colour plate of Nebuchadnezzar which looked as if it must have inspired Boyd's series of tiles illustrating that biblical story. So I showed it to her.

(I later found that I was wrong about Bundanoon. Boyd's home is at Bundanon near Nowra, much further south.)

I asked if she lived in Canberra, and she explained that she had been there to attend the funeral of her eighteen-year-old great niece. She said it had been her great wish to get to the funeral but, because she lived in a retirement village and was not well, she had not known how she would be able to manage the journey alone. "I prayed and said, 'Well, Lord, I leave it up to you'." Half an hour later the woman who was in the seat in front of us, also wearing an orthopaedic collar, had walked into her room and hearing her news, had offered to accompany her.

They both belong to the Little Company of Mary, religious sisters whose order once owned the Little Company Guest House, as it now is, the resort in Leura. She told me her name was Sister Venya and that this was the name of a male French missionary who had died for the faith in China. She said the members of her order are not nuns but religious sisters.

"Our order was begun by Mother Margaret Potter in England last century. She really began it to help pray for the dying. We work with the dying and many of us are nursing sisters. Our founder went to Rome for a while and, in fact, she stayed on there and never returned."

I said that this must have been difficult for a young order.

"Well, yes it was. There were many disaffections and dissensions, but we survived."

She spoke about grief, loss and joy. These things are much on my mind lately as I struggle with my grief at Lily's withdrawal from me since she left Jack, and the shock of his lies.

Sister Venya, sitting dry-eyed beside me as the golden country rolled by, spoke of the death of her sister's granddaughter. Then of the death of her friend's son. He was found by his mother, hanging in his room, when she called him to dinner. He left no note, was in the grip of no unhappy love affair. His mother had picked him up from work and he, after joking about her driving, had gone downstairs to his room while she was cooking, and killed himself.

Sister Venya had known her friend, his mother, since she was a young nurse in her care.

"I was standing at the top of the stairs. I used to go there sometimes to meet the girls coming on duty. I saw her coming up the stairs and I said 'Jen, you've got stars in your eyes!' She said 'Have I Sister? Well, I've met somebody'."

My own grief was put into perspective listening to this. But I did remark that we are continually being tested and that, as one grows older, the challenges continue and are at a level one can only just bear without collapsing. Hearty agreement from Sister Venya.

As the train jolted into Strathfield, the sister in front came to help Sister Venya to her feet. Together they walked out with a smile and a wave. I sat there going over the conversation. It had been like sitting next to a bunch of violets. I remembered that the phrase 'the odour of sanctity' comes from the story that when a saint's tomb is opened, the scent of violets rises up. I am not saying I sat beside a saint but there was sanctity in the air. And restored I went on my way.

I'm cooking for Easter.

There will be eight of us. Hence the cook-up. Hugh, Cathy and Sophia Rose will be staying here with me. Ghilly, John and their two daughters will sleep at a motel as they did at Christmas, but they will eat with us. They are due tomorrow morning.

Nan's making us a beef casserole. She starts by frying the meat for at least three times as long a I do. This concentrates the flavour and caramelises it. It stops it becoming a stew. She chops the vegetables (except for the onions) into long shreds so that they can go in at the last and keep their shape and flavour.

I made a boiled chocolate raisin cake and a 'Guard's pudding' using some of the strawberry jam I made last week. This is a good pudding. It is Arabella Boxer's recipe.

3 eggs
½ tsp bicarbonate of soda
3 oz butter
3 oz castor sugar
5 oz fresh breadcrumbs
5 tbsp strawberry jam

Beat the eggs well. Dissolve soda in a teaspoon of cold water. Melt butter. Stir these gradually into the other ingredients, mixing well. Spoon into a buttered mould and steam for 2 hours. Serve with rich custard and/or cream or ice cream. This is enough for 5 – 6 people.

Lamb is traditional at Easter so we're having a stuffed boned leg. I'm making rhubarb crumble and a raspberry coulis to have with a sorbet.

The menu is a challenge because John's allergic to garlic. Ghilly, sceptical of this, fed him some secretly and he had nightmares all night.

Cathy can't eat curry, chilli or garlic, because she's breast-feeding. Garlic makes some breast-fed babies scream if their mothers eat it. But Italian babies, they say, don't mind it. I find this hard to believe. How can there be a simply geographically-based allergy? Could it be that garlic-eating mothers produce non-allergic babies? Babies hate coffee in breast milk.

I've chopped up about forty cloves in the blender so it can be sprinkled on the food separately.

A letter fell from a pile beside my bed. It was from Patricia, the friend I stayed with in Canberra this week. She had written to me from Bangkok where she was artist-in-residence at Silpakorn University last year.

> I feel like I am running around with my head chopped off – it takes a long time to do nothing – it will be good for me – change my way of thinking. I have a small room with toilet and hand shower. The bed is rock hard – let us hope my body adjusts – I have a small area

to paint in but I shall work from an easel – give my back a chance to come back to normal. From where I am sitting I can see the Grand Palace – it tries to glitter in the smog but looks like a tarnished old lady. There were so many greys the first few days I was beginning to wonder what had happened to the blue skies (aftermath of the hurricane in the Philippines). But today it is a *wonderful* summers day. Unfortunately I sat on my sunglasses – trust they can fix them. Going to paint thinly, everything, as I am broke for a while – light washes – I have asked for some stretchers to be made – will they ever materialise? It is a festival of night today – you float candles on the river so nasty spirits float away leaving only good ones behind – am lighting them for all my friends. Kate I read *Mad Meg* over the last few days – a great book – and now on to Lawrence Durrell's *Alexandrian Quartet* that should keep me going. However there are bookshops here this time around. Weekends I shall sit in a comfortable chair at the Oriental or Sheraton reading the English newspapers – a small amount of civilized living in a week.

It is a mistake to think these residencies are a kind of working holiday and always easy. The places seem so romantic, such a dream for an artist, but in reality, with no air conditioning and few conveniences, they are often unbelievably uncomfortable and lonely. One day the Australia Council, with the best will in the world, will find they have lost somebody who has killed herself from loneliness or depression.

Once I nearly went mad, sitting each day in a room with a blanket stuffed under the door to block the cigarette smoke from the asthmatic administrator in her lavish office next door. I lay on a broken single bed, a naked light globe overhead, no radio, no lamp, no bed linen or blankets at first, and no food for three days. The contrast between the office and the place for the writer-in-residence could not have been more marked. But since this was funded by the local taxpayers, I had to hold my tongue.

A young playwright once told me of a residency she did in Paris. She suffered such colossal loneliness that she lasted six weeks and fled. Each evening she'd lean out of her window and look down. A young man would always be there, standing alone looking out at the street. She said, "I thought, 'Don't look up because, if you do, we're both doomed'."

Sarah, a poet friend, took her partner and baby daughter to Rome in the height of the summer. She wrote early in the morning while the baby's father took her out in her pusher into the streets full of steps. When he came home they would just swelter out the day trying not to kill each other. They fled.

The local embassies do little or nothing to help as they do not see it as their role and are anyhow too busy. The whole thing needs rethinking. The worry is that, if matters are investigated, the whole scheme will be judged as just too difficult and will be abandoned. So I suppose it is better that residencies lurch on in the way they at present do. Some people enjoy them.

7th April, Easter Sunday. Leura.

The Easter egg hunt went awry. I couldn't remember where Ghilly and John had left their bag of eggs, so I could only put out two I had and a bag of chocolates Hugh and Cathy had stashed in the soup tureen. It was not enough for Stephanie and Donna. Ghilly, puzzled, asked "But where are our eggs?" Cathy ran to their car and Ghilly to theirs to find more. While I tried to keep the girls round the back by calling "Look under the pines. He usually leaves some there. Try the watering can," Ghilly threw a bag of eggs around the front garden. Hopping from bush to bush the girls soon found them, with John trying to make sure Donna wasn't too far behind her older sister.

Then we all went to church, upstairs with the organist because of the crowd. In front of us a young father held two wriggling girls of about four or five – and their dolls – wedged firmly in the crook of each elbow. When he prayed sitting, he held one child under a bent leg thrust out in front, as he had no pew or chair to lean his arms on. She lay there lolling under her father's body, swinging an armless, naked doll by a leg and sucking her thumb.

A ginger-haired elderly nun in a blouse and sky blue sleeveless jumper stood beside the organ and sang sweetly. The organist wore a purple dress. She had run in late, up the stairs past us, saying "Please let me pass. Excuse me!"

Men stood outside and poked their heads in through the back windows. This reminded me of Africa. When I went to church there, it was so crowded that there were half as many outdoors as there were inside. Women in bright dresses, wearing scarves of the same fabric, holding small girls in frilly bright pink dresses and small boys in tiny adult clothes, strolled up and down the aisles on their way to buy sweets and chips from the vendors standing outside in the sun. It looked like a dress parade. The band played ukeleles and everyone sang jazz and negro spirituals. It was a cross between a concert, a fair, a mass, a picnic, a bonanza.

Cathy's sisters came to lunch. Four of them. They remind me of a fairy story about ravens who turn into princesses. Maria, the youngest, is very blonde. Jo's got black hair. Martina is a redhead and Karen is also blonde. We sat in the garden and John lay in the hammock with his girls and we drank red wine. From the back verandah I took a photo of the circle on the lawn peering out from under their hats. The sisters drove off in a red car in time for *Pride and Prejudice.* It is the last episode tonight.

Hugh made Donna laugh by being Rex the sheep dog who needs convincing to let Babe come to stay. Cathy, sitting in a wicker chair, fed the baby and was Babe. "My mother called us Babe." Then Hugh hid his mouth behind his hand and became Mum, the dog who mothers Babe. Donna screamed with joy. She calls him "Funny Man." She knelt on the couch shrieking "Funny Man do some more!"

8th April, Monday. Leura.

A picnic at the caves. Hugh grilled fresh sardine fillets and chops, while we sat under a tree and opened the wine. The bowerbird's bower wasn't in the bush when we crouched down to look. Sometimes it's there, sometimes it's not. I never give up hope.

At home in the afternoon some drank coffee, some read, some

played with children. I made 'Mussels Portuguese' with saffron a friend had given me. Hugh and Cathy went to Bon Ton with their Danish friends.

When they came back Hugh asked Ghilly to teach him how to sing 'Amazing Grace'. He said "It's a good song." Last time I heard him learning a song it was 'Belsen was a Gas'. He was in a punk band called 'The Accountants'.

He stood strong like a tree beside Ghilly, singing bravely. She stopped him. "No. Let your jaw drop. Use your soft palate."

"I don't know anything about that. What is it?"

She explained that it goes right round the back of your mouth, and to let it resonate.

The affection between the man and the woman. The way they trusted each other. Hugh was like a man alone on a hill singing to people in the valley below.

9th April, Tuesday. Leura.

We went to the baker's and got a lot of bread. The Leura village baker makes a rye sourdough that is good with marmalade, especially Rose's lime.

The woman who served us said it had been ugly over Easter. I thought she meant it had been busy but she said people were impatient. They bullied and were tense. Hugh said it's the traffic that drives them mad. To get here takes so long at holiday times.

Sophia Rose is doing that dolphin kind of talk that babies do. Sometimes she gets a run at her voice and you can see how thrilled she is at getting her throat to work. Sometimes she laughs. Cathy says she's been told to make the same sounds to show the baby that she is understood.

When she's laid on her stomach in the bath, she first turns her face away from the water and then kicks and swims. We use the big bath for her and Cathy sits on a child's low chair beside it. After her bath she sleeps. The air here makes everybody sleep.

So that's Easter. The breaking of the fast.

10th April, Wednesday. Leura.

Marisa and Sam are coming on the train at noon. Now that Easter's over there's a damp silver silence outside with the red trees set like rubies on a bracelet. I am cooking beetroot risotto. The recipe came today from Rhyll who runs Pigdon's restaurant in Carlton. Here's how it's made:

1 bunch beetroot
1 bunch baby beetroot
150 ml good quality olive oil
1 onion, finely diced
1 carrot, finely diced
1 stick celery, finely diced
1 sprig rosemary, finely chopped
6 cups Arborio rice
1.5 litres chicken stock
reserved beet leaves
butter
salt and pepper
grated parmesan (to serve)

Trim both beetroots and cook in enough water to cover them. Peel beetroot, grate large beets and leave baby ones whole. Reserve cooking liquid and set beets aside.

Bring stock to boil and set over low heat.

Heat olive oil and add onion, carrot, celery and rosemary. Cook on low for 5 minutes. Add Arborio rice stirring with a wooden spoon to coat with oil. Add warm stock, a little at a time after each addition has been absorbed, taking care to stir all the time so risotto doesn't stick. Once absorbed add grated beet, 2 cups beetroot liquid and finally baby beets. Risotto should have a flowing consistency and not be chalky in the middle.

A few minutes before risotto is cooked, add beet leaves, salt, pepper and a spoonful of butter. Top with parmesan shavings.

Later

Sitting at the table eating, Marisa has been telling me how to preserve the orange-fleshed brown-topped huge mushrooms that grow here. She looked at me quizzically when I said "You're lucky to have all this knowledge. It's wonderful your mother taught you so much." She gave a short laugh.

"My mother couldn't cook when she came to Australia. In Trieste she took us out for coffee in the morning with her friends. We had lunch in a café. At six at night we'd meet her friends and go to a bar and have hot chocolate. We'd wait for my father to finish work at eight o'clock, which was when people finished there. Then we'd go to a restaurant and eat."

Then, after a bite or two, she added, "My mother taught herself to cook from an Australian book. When our neighbours gave us rhubarb we cooked the leaves and threw away the stems!"

"But the leaves are poisonous," I said.

She said that they'd tasted so horrid they'd only taken a mouthful.

11th April, Thursday. Leura.

"Grandma, will you please stop snoring?" Sam asked, lying beside me this morning. We slept together so that Marisa could have his room. Two pillows between the length of us made a buffer from his kicking and helped me sleep.

After breakfast Marisa set out a blue rag rug in the sunroom and, looking out into the red dogwood, the bird cherries and the apples, put on her headphones and listened to her tape. I don't know if the possession of a calm mind and a serene spirit can help people recover from cancer. There are many theories, beliefs and hopes and so little is proved. But it seems to make sense that if the immune system is rested, it can better help to fight disease. And if this is so, does it mean that stress can help cause cancer?

Hugh asked John about this at Easter. John said that nothing has been proved though there is a lot of anecdotal evidence to support the belief.

This dull writing is driving me mad because I'm worried about Lily.

12th April, Friday. Leura.

Autumn is creeping in here like a red sleuth. Red and green parrots were pecking and flitting in the apple trees yesterday when I was lying, sucking a pen, trying to write a poem about strawberry jam.

Marisa, Sam and I walked to Katoomba today. Marisa was always ahead, hurling herself up the hills, tiny, red-haired, wearing my apple-green angora beret. She liked the Paragon Café. She had a caffe latte and we had vanilla milkshakes. Then we went further in to look at the art deco cocktail lounge. A man dressed in a black suit and tie, black hair sleeked back, was drinking coffee at a small round table. With one leg crossed over the other, a shiny black shoe glittering below the brass table, he looked like an actor about to start in an art deco film.

We walked to Mr Todarello's because Marisa was keen to buy lettuce so that I can make a good lunch when the publisher comes tomorrow. She spoke Italian to Mrs Todarello.

On the way home, looking at the blue infinity stretching away past the neat lines of houses, she told me how to make a dish of roast root vegetables.

Marisa's roast root vegetables

Slice a mixture of vegetables into thick rings or pieces: carrots, parsnips, sweet potato, butternut pumpkin, celeriac, onions (red onions are good for this). Place them in a baking dish on top of branches or sprigs of fresh oregano and other herbs. (You can use chopped herbs.) Sprinkle chopped garlic through and over this.

Squeeze the juice from ripe halved tomatoes into another vessel and lay the tomatoes near the top.

Cut small egg plants in halves and insert them, cut side up, among the vegetables. Strew more chopped herbs and garlic over the dish, and pour olive oil on top. Canola or safflower oil can be used.

Bake in a very slow oven for 3 – 4 hours depending on how many vegetables are in the pan. If it is piled high, it may take 4 hours.

The aim is to get the vegetables to caramelise without burning. Give them plenty of time but don't allow them to lose their shape.

To ensure this make the slices about the thickness of a finger and cut the softer vegetables thicker than this. The trick is to keep their shape and stop them getting too soft.

When ready lift each piece onto a big white platter. Heat the drippings in the pan with 1 tbsp sugar, and at the last moment add 1 tbsp balsamic vinegar. Stir well and pour over the dish.

Serve either warm or at room temperature with good bread and a green salad. If you wish you can serve separately a jug of yoghurt mixed through with chopped garlic and chopped Italian parsley.

The bread is used to mop up the juice.

I asked if potatoes could go into the dish. Marisa paused, put her head on one side and considered, as this was obviously a new idea.

"No, I wouldn't use them. You could roast them separately with rosemary and serve them with the other vegetables, but I wouldn't cook them together."

It is always a mistake to assume that Italian recipes, which seem almost thrown together in the most casual way, are unstructured. They are anything but that. They are extremely subtle and refined, although they may use things that are not expensive. They ought not to be altered much at all. Almost biblical in seriousness and authority, they don't take well to alteration.

When we got home Marisa ate a carrot and packed. We walked to the train.

On the way back I called on Nan and Phil who gave me curried egg sandwiches and tea. They are the ultimate insomniacs. They could run a submarine between them. A light is always on in one or other of their bedrooms. Sleeplessness in old age is almost endemic it seems. It's horrible, walking around at three in the morning, drinking tea, waiting for dawn, exhausted, dreading the day.

Nan walked me to the gate and plucked a branch from a maple. The leaves, peachy pink and big, I put on my head like a veil and said "I'm Autumn." She smiled and walked back down the drive.

13th April, Saturday. Leura.

The house nearly burnt down this morning. When I was raking the ashes a few small hot coals turned up, so I decided to get the stove going immediately and put in paper, a cardboard box of kindling and two logs. Then I went to get more wood and some herbs for the Italian dish and left the stove door open. I heard a thud as I was breaking off the stalks of oregano. Not running, but not moving slowly either, I lugged the wood indoors. Light was running up the wall, flaring. I called out "Oh God don't let it be bad!". The box had fallen out and was burning on the hearth amongst the washing drying round the fireplace. I flung a towel on the fire. The room was full of black smoke. Opening the window I kept thinking that if I were overcome by smoke I wouldn't be able to fight the fire. After a while I got the burning towel into the fireplace with the burning logs and kindling. A lesson. I would have sworn I would never leave the house with the stove door open. Would have put money on it.

My lunch guest, the publisher, has not turned up. My fault probably as I was rattled on the phone, because of the fire, and said I'd call back. But when I did, leaving a message that he was expected for lunch, it was a bit late.

14th April, Sunday. Leura.

To church this morning in my new Armani brown silk-velvet skirt.

I raked chestnuts and lugged them home in barrows and big bags for Sam to set up his stall next time he comes. He'd said it was chestnut time and he'd like to go and gather them at Tom and Jude's. But I'd said "No, it's Anzac Day they're ready." I was wrong. Last year he set up a card table on the grass verge and a notice he'd made: 'Chestnuts $1 one bag. $2 two bags. $3 three bags.' (I had asked him how much he was going to charge for two bags if one bag was one dollar, and his answer was logical though not what I'd expected.) People waved from their cars. Some stopped, some took photographs, some bought. He had a rake, a barrow, two tiny rush-bottom chairs and, on one of the days, his friend Odile to help him. He sat there for three days, five hours a day.

Things like this determine careers. My father and his brother Doug, when they were young, gathered a barrow of peaches and wheeled it around the streets to sell them. Their mother spotted them and was horrified. When in his fifties Doug bought a greengrocery, I wondered whether the barrow of peaches was involved.

The house smells of roasted vegetables left over from my solitary lunch yesterday. There's only so much one person can eat.

With autumn now raving, lying and watching the trees in the sun is like living inside a cathedral. Droplets of shining water were caught where the leaves join the branches of the bird cherry nearest to the day bed. No other tree around was like this so it may have been its sap shining. I can't understand it. A gift shining against the azure blue. Then white scraps of clouds appeared, tore apart and dissolved in the blue. I fell asleep in my boots.

Later

Pausing at the gate, a stranger, an elderly stout man with a handlebar moustache and a dog to match, addressed me:

Season of mists and mellow fruitfulness,
Close bosom-friend of the maturing sun;
Conspiring with him how to load and bless
With fruit the vines that round the thatch-eaves run;
To bend with apples the mossed cottage-trees,
And fill all fruit with ripeness to the core;
To swell the gourd, and plump the hazel shells
With a sweet kernel; to set budding more,
And still more, later flowers for the bees...

Then he added, "That's Keats." I said "Yes, I know." I would have to say that.

21st April, Sunday. Leura.

I've set up a card table in the sunroom to work on in the sun. Outside the sun pours down on the trees, raving, a red and holy bedlam. A currawong flew down to the rock for a heel of sourdough bread I'd thrown out. A magpie standing beside the bread raised its head to the sky and began to sing.

Yesterday I came home from minding Sophia while her mother went to university. Andrew, who was best man at Hugh and Cathy's wedding, was coming to dinner so I bought racks of lamb to roast. The butcher in Newtown, seeing my anxiety as I tried to give the baby a bottle sitting on a bench in his shop, asked if I'd like a cup of coffee or a glass of water. I wanted cranberry sauce and mustard to paste on the meat but he had none, not being a grocer. So it was back to the supermarket with its silver posts at the entrance that bar prams. I watched a mother with twins simply lift one of the posts from its base and wheel in the pram, so I did the same. Everything is a challenge with a pram or a wheelchair.

I fed the baby in a small park. A man there was standing to attention, staring into the sun as if being inspected by a general. When I looked next he had obviously been ordered to stand at ease so, legs apart, hands behind his back, he stood relaxed, waiting I suppose to be dismissed. Mothers lifted their children up to the top of the slippery dip and caught them at the bottom.

Two young women greeted each other and sat down, while their babies, both in navy-blue overalls, rushed stumbling towards each other. When one sat down unexpectedly, with a thud of padded pants, the other, propelled perhaps by the force of his speed, veered off and kept going until he too thudded to a halt.

Sophia, lying between a net bag of lemons and another of red capsicum, grew hot and cried all the way home as I tore along, cooing and thrumming like an excited pigeon.

25th April, Thursday. Newcastle.

Today is Anzac Day. The school choir sang 'Let us now praise famous men' while the parents sat in the sun on chairs on the tennis courts. Three cadets stood with their guns, heads bowed, hands folded over the rifle butts. Father Graham gave a speech about mateship, a fair go and compassion. His white surplice waved in the breeze which ruffled his grey hair. Beside us sat the junior school, legs crossed, boys in blue souwesters, girls in round straw hats.

The small boy next to us seemed to be dreaming. Too young to read and follow the service, he pulled at his thumb nail and when a prayer was announced, put his hands together obediently and bowed his fair curly head. I thought that if we hadn't won the last World War he'd possibly be being taught Fascism today and chanting something abominable.

We sang *Advance Australia Fair*. Then two girls in year 8 played the violin and a boy sang 'And the band played Waltzing Matilda', while the wind blew his voice away and the microphone failed and recovered, over and over.

Then we all sang 'Oh God our help in ages past' and tears burnt my lids when we came to the lines

Time, like an ever-rolling stream, bears all its sons away.
They fly forgotten as a dream dies at the opening day.

I thought we all too will be swept away, even the children. And I thought of those men who fought at El Alamein and who hurled hand grenades into trenches full of other soldiers. The horror of war and the grief of it.

Surely I can forgive somebody who badmouths me to our friends. If we can't stop hating and taking revenge, we'll keep fighting and small wars will break out, then larger ones, and so on and so on, for ever and ever.

When we were dismissed the children marched into school, led by the colour party of girls in army uniforms, their stiff arms swinging backwards and forwards above their clenched fists, their ponytails hanging down their backs.

Ghilly and I bought corned beef to make an Anzac dinner: boiled beef and carrots, with boiled potatoes and parsley sauce. I know soldiers didn't get exactly this but they did have tinned corned beef, so it seemed the nearest thing. It seems selfish to think of food after such a service but the living eat. Even after funerals they eat.

I could not have been given a better example of healing and forgiveness than the book Ghilly lent me last night, Jan Ruff O'Hearne's autobiography *Fifty Years of Silence*. She, along with her friends, was made a prostitute in a brothel for Japanese soldiers in Indonesia during the last war. They were called 'comfort women'. Jan describes the opening night of the brothel and the way she begged.

Her daughter Carol is a friend of Ghilly's. She knew nothing of this part of her mother's life until she was handed a notebook before getting on a plane to Darwin one day. It was the only way Jan could think of to tell her. Carol cried so much on the plane everyone was bewildered.

Jan laid a wreath at the Adelaide War Memorial on Sunday, 8th March 1992, the fiftieth anniversary of the surrender of Java to Japanese troops. That year she decided to come forward after the first Korean woman, Mrs Kim Hak Sun, had told her story about being made a comfort woman. The Japanese government had made no apology to these women and Jan thought it might help sway opinion, and make Japan take more notice, if a European woman spoke out. She told of her experience of being one of the seven young women at the House of the Seven Seas, the Japanese officers' club and brothel in Semarang.

The Japanese government finally responded to the outcry about comfort women and Jan was a witness at the international public hearing which began in Tokyo on 9th December 1992.

Many at the hearing cried when they heard what she and the others had suffered. A Chinese woman fell backwards and fainted after she had spoken of the crimes she had endured. After this uproar Jan spoke, saying that she had forgiven the Japanese for what they had done. Twenty South Korean women spoke next. They were dressed in white, their colour of mourning. Then a particularly heart-rending story of torture was told by a North Korean woman. As she was speaking the group from South Korea crept forward and surrounded her, and when she had finished they embraced her. They had not known that women from all over the country had been forced into prostitution.

A group of women under the name of 'Atomic Bomb Sufferers', survivors of Hiroshima, came up to talk to Jan. "Now we know that we were not the only people who suffered" they said, putting their arms around her.

A feeling of peace came over me in the presence of these women. They gave me presents and postcards, and I gave them handkerchiefs printed with Australian wildflowers.

Then, at the end of the week, to show she had come to Japan, not with hatred but with forgiveness, Jan and Carol made a 'wreath of forgiveness' from Australian wildflowers and Jan laid it at the Chidorigafuchi, the Memorial for the Unknown Soldier, in a park. She had invited people to the ceremony and along with the Dutch ambassador and several human rights groups came a bus load of former Japanese soldiers from the Second World War. They welcomed her with flowers, books and gifts. She said:

"Today I am laying a wreath at your memorial in Tokyo, with the Japanese people standing at my side. The wreath is a sign of peace and forgiveness. A sign of hope for the future of the world, the future of our children.

"I hope that after fifty years we have learnt the lesson that we are putting the war behind us and that we can work together towards a world of peace. A world without hatred and fear, without war and violence, but rather a world of peace and understanding, friendship and love and freedom."

Some of the elderly ex-soldiers came forward and read speeches and prayers. Some of these men were Christians and Jan says "I was very touched by one man who gave a moving talk in broken English and ended by reading that beautiful psalm, Psalm 51, with the words 'My sin is always before me.'

Then Jan held out her hands to the ex-soldiers and prayed the peace prayer of St Francis of Assisi. Her translator, whose father had been an officer in the Imperial Army, began to cry. They concluded the speech together, holding hands. She writes

> I could sense an intense oneness with these Japanese people, present here for this simple ceremony.

26th April, Friday. Newcastle.

Down at Lily Pond picnic area, wattle birds are calling Qwark! Qwark! Men here, working on the house extension, are hammering. They begin at seven. "Fair go mate!" was the first thing I heard.

Last night Phil Graham, a colleague of John's, came to dinner. He said he's been writing an essay on hyperbolic logic. I asked what that was and was told it is the sort of logic Descartes used until he came to doubt everything except 'I think therefore I am.'

Ghilly, drinking tea with me on her bed this morning, said

"I know you like that sort of talk, but do you ever watch the Simpsons? Well, do you know the groan Marge lets out from time to time?" (And here she groaned.) "Well, that's how I feel when a discussion of philosophy begins. I am just not suited to it. I am much more interested in what kind of an old age I'll have and will I have enough money to buy some good jewellery. We used to have that sort of talk by our teachers in Adult Matric. Do you remember? I always found it very irritating."

She makes me laugh.

During dinner John read us the passage from Elizabeth Jolley's *The George's Wife* in which she speaks of healing.

> To the questions, is there a Balm and is there a Physician, my answer is yes. There is trust, there is courage and there is kindness. These are the ingredients. And anyone can be the Physician.

I had read this to him this morning, following him round the garden while he hosed wearing his shorts and nothing else. He said it had been too early for him then and the passage had just perplexed him.

29th April, Monday. Newcastle.

I am going to come and live here. Yesterday, as the cathedral choir was singing the Gloria, it was as if a shaft of light fell down on me. I thought, I am going to move. All weekend there has been music. Jessie Norman is singing on the radio now. At Evensong the choir sang the Nunc Dimittis, the stars appearing outside.

Lord, now lettest thou thy servant depart in peace, according to thy word, for mine eyes have seen thy salvation.

Then John and I came home and watched 'The Choir' on television and ate scrambled eggs full of parsley.

I was alone for a while over the weekend as Ghilly and John went to a conference at Kirkton House, somewhere in the Hunter valley, on Saturday. There was a storm that night and I was sure somebody was walking over the roof, so I got into Donna's bunk among the dolls.

The neighbours, who gave me a lift, told me the names of their children, sitting in the back, were Zoe and Alexander. Paul then said,

"I have a second cousin I haven't seen for a few years. And I hear he's got two children about the same age as our two, and he's given them the same names. He didn't know our kids' names and we didn't know theirs."

There are strange stories like this, particularly about twins separated at birth.

Ghilly and I are going for a walk and then to town. She's to fetch the tiles the builders need to begin on the bathroom. I am going in to teach.

May

11th May, Saturday. Leura.

After floods in the north and big rains here, pink clouds passed across a silver sky this morning. Now a plain blue sky.

For some reason I've been walking around the house in quiet despair, staring out at a wretched garden.

I got some consolation from reading, in Thomas Moore's *Care of the Soul*, that Renaissance doctors believed the essence of each one of us originates as a star in the heavens. In the 1980s, the ex-Dominican Matthew Fox wrote "Every element of our body exploded in a supernova five and a half million years ago and we are literally stardust." I used to think, when I was young, that people are like stars in that we can only see part of one another, and there is a whole mysterious unseen area we can never share with one another, even if we live together half a lifetime.

A massacre has occurred at Port Arthur. There hardly seems a way to understand how it could happen. The fact that it happened at a place where evil had been makes it seem more powerful. Some places, like some people, hold evil from events. What dark star could murder like this? I keep bursting into tears.

Thomas Moore writes about the sacredness of life. He also says that care of the soul needs our appreciation of the way depression can be a gift. Grey, blue and black are some of the colours we can have in our souls and we must observe the whole range of colours he says. And we must guard against the denial of death when dealing with depression. More and more I see that I learn most from times of suffering. And I just hate this.

It may be that the feeling of being betrayed, the shock and then the anger, have now turned to melancholy. I haven't got much to be sad about. The house stands. I could garden if I had the energy. Everybody, except my sister-in-law Jan, is well in our family. Some friends are left. If my hair had fallen out and were growing back now, I'd be very happy. The fact that it hasn't fallen out (and so doesn't need to grow back) should be making me just as happy. So what's the matter? Don't know. Can't say. I don't want to get out of bed.

It was a good thing yesterday that there were two reasons to get up. Tom Folwell was packing up thirty paintings to send to a gallery in Noumea and had invited Nan and me down to see them. The paintings are of sheds, birds and the sea, serene as pale clouds. Nan and I were calmed and made happy watching as he brought them out one by one.

Jeff, the man who gardens, was coming so I made some upside-down apple cakes. He dug up the parts of the garden I don't know what to do with. Gardening has several phases of learning and the first is knowing how, what, where and when to plant. It has taken me ten years to grasp this. After the early planning and planting I leaned back and let things go, thinking that the job was more or less finished. But now it's obvious that maintenance is another matter and requires a different apprenticeship. I never like to take anything out. So unruly roughage rages everywhere and I stand amongst it, looking bewildered.

Nan did a walk in my garden when I asked for advice. She said *everything* but the shrubs and trees needed to be dug out. This was so upsetting I went straight to bed. But now it's done it is better although I hate these bald beds. Like empty beds in a hospital they seem wasted.

What I really like is an orderly mess. I don't think I risk the depression sometimes found in people who are either very untidy or extremely neat.

Phil is launching my book on East Africa next Friday. We were talking this over by their fire last week, and then we discussed journalists, and how to talk to them. Phil advises prefacing all talk to journalists with "This is off the record. After we have finished speaking, you can tell me what you'd like to quote and then, and only then, will I tell you what you *can* quote. If you don't like this, then..." And he mimed putting down the phone.

I have never met anyone who can listen the way Phil listens to a person. It must be his training as a judge added to a natural talent. It has the effect of making one fastidious about what is said. The truth, although he never asks for it, becomes suddenly crucial. Even a small exaggeration becomes all at once a blaring lie and you struggle to regain balance and speak with greater accuracy. No doctor, lover or examiner has ever paid such attention to what I said. Listening, an art so few have, costs nothing but is one of the hardest things to do. It is also the most loving and complimentary thing we can do for one another. I am going to try to stay silent whenever somebody is telling me something.

18th May, Saturday. Leura.

A 8 p.m. last night I went to see the baker bake. Warwick is a man in love with bread. I've seen people in love with wood, birds, music and even musical instruments but not bread. As I walked in, a man was grinding coffee beans in a huge machine with deafening noise. He stopped and we shook hands. Paul, hair tied up in a pink and blue scarf, pointed the way into the bakery's main room. A magnum of champagne with about a third left was on the desk. That day there had been a column in the *Herald* saying they were one of the top three sourdough bakeries in the state so Warwick is celebrating with his bakers.

By 1.30 a.m. I had learnt how to roll a long loaf, a round loaf, to knot a roll and cover it in poppyseed, and how hard all this is on the feet. The five men wore favourite shoes: some runners, some Swiss hiking boots. By the end of the night I was shuffling like a bear on a chain. Warwick made oblong pizza from the dough with artichokes, dried tomatoes, cheese and tomato salsa poured on, made for the shop by the gallon. It is roasted tomatoes; not just halved as usual, rather sliced up mixed with oregano, oil, a drop of balsamic, some garlic and slowly roasted over hours. It is a secret and good. I rang up today and ordered nine kilos of tomatoes to begin at once. We stood up to eat; there were no chairs except at the desk. The ovens reach the ceiling.

The dried apricot and cashew brioche fell flat. "Something like this always goes wrong every time we have a visitor" Justin said.

I stuck labels on about a hundred loaves or so, then took a swig of champagne about 11 p.m. wondering how I'd last. But a second wind came. The white dough lay like a young polar bear sleeping curled on the huge white table that was like an iceflow. They cut and weighed it loaf by loaf and rolled it out by hand. Two loaves at a time, a hand for each loaf. I laboured on, dough sticking to my hands, dipping them in the water bucket they used. The machine hooked the dough, batch after batch. Warwick ran his fingers through the bags of organic flour, pure as ground ivory. Ecstatic as a miser with his gold. "Feel it, just feel it, these people are geniuses! Wendy and Paul make this at Gunnedah." These little pockets of excellence exist all over the country.

Warwick's loaves cost $3.70 but weigh 700 grams. Supermarket loaves weigh 400 grams but are bigger in size and have hard fats, hydrologized, any old fats. Warwick uses only virgin olive oil and spring or filtered water. The men worked on. I sank my hands into a sink three and half metres long. I longed to dangle my feet in the lovely warm suds. Flour stuck to my face. I kept wiping it with the apron Warwick had tied onto me. It was white and on the bib was printed a green pea pod, a red heart and a wrapped lolly like a tiny bonbon. His wife Vanessa made it for him he said; a code. His name is Lolly and hers is Pod.

They have two small children who were in the car waiting for him to say goodnight when Vanessa, seven months pregnant, called in.

Later, I heard that young Justin had children and that Erin with his big brown curly ponytail, who I thought was a teenager, has a six-week-old baby girl Xalia. "It's Xalia with an X," said Justin. "Did you tell her it's an X?"

"I must say bakers seem to be good breeders," I said.

"It's all the yeast," Warwick said. "Now only young Paul over there needs to start."

Paul was making croissants, custard and sultana cinnamon rolls, chocolate croissants, apricot danish and other patisserie. I rolled some croissants with him when he showed me how. Outside the crescent moon shone down each time I went to the toilet, inside more rolling, baking, rolling. The patisserie dough is made with white organic flour and boxes of butter. We unwrapped a box and plopped it into the dough machine to soften. The secret I learnt is to mix 80% of the butter with flour first and then put that into the yeast dough. It is folded around the butter like a lover in bed. Then it rests 12 hours in the fridge before the rolling and folding begins. Oh I could go on for ever.

The first thing I noticed was the backs of the men. They were all like tables, so strong. It is of course the rolling and lifting – there are no women bakers there, although Julia comes for patisseries on some nights and is an expert, Warwick said.

At one in the morning Warwick was saying to Erin, "Oh they aren't bursting!" as he peered into the oven with the rye loaves revolving under a faint light. They are slit in a tree-shaped drawing on top by Erin and are meant not only to burst up from the cut, but to rise out from the pattern in jagged crusts like cliffs. We had to watch every few minutes and to suddenly turn down the heat, pause, let the temperature fall, and then make it roar and race again. This causes the bursting, crusting, splitting and other thickenings of the crust – all new to me.

I saw the trays of brioches, all good but slumped a bit in the middle, about to go to the bin and called ardently, "Let me take some home for toast." So I loaded nine into bags and the neighbours can have some. They are as big as loaves of bread, and covered in light brown sugar. Now I wish I had gathered more.

Mark's ducks might get some, Warwick said. $100 of dough out to the ducks and bins. All my frugality rose in desperation.

Outside the cold air, the bright stars and into the taxi laden with brioches and home. I could barely walk. I lay in the bath smelling of vanilla (all the custard in the patisserie). I want to learn to make something, one thing, really well. To perfect it and make it each time Sam comes. So he will treasure it. But the work involved, all that twisting of butter and so forth and washing up, just daunts me.

Today I walked down to look at the window of loaves and glossy little cakes. I will never waste as much as a heel of good bread again.

Later I was telling Nan about the bakery. Her family were bakers. "My father used tons and tons of potatoes to make bread in 1927. It intrigues me because I never did discover why they used potatoes. Perhaps they were cheaper than flour – they extended the flour.

"I remember men sitting down in white overalls on boxes peeling boiled potatoes. They had a big vat like a beer barrel into which they put the potatoes when they'd peeled them. They were still warm."

"And then what happened to the potatoes Nan?"

"I don't know Katie, I was only five."

I stood up to go and said, "My word Nan, you got diamonds from bread."

She laughed. I said this because months ago she showed me a magnificent diamond and pearl Victorian necklace she was sending to Christies in London to sell. Along with this was a ruby and diamond brooch and diamond rings. She explained that with two daughters she could not chop up the necklace and divide it so the whole lot were sold and the money given to her girls. Then I saw her wedding photograph, showing her wearing the necklace. She said, "Oh it's no use having a thing like this now. My mother wore it to the pictures with a friend and they were followed. So she put it in the bank vault and I only wore it when I was a bride."

And as for those fox's eyes, the golden stars that rained their brightness on Thursday night, when Bill in his dressing gown walked me across the road after dinner. We looked up, and they were there. As if hands full of gold had been spilt on a blue-black shroud. And every night the trees, the animals see these while we shrug the blankets closer. Or fight, yawn, or make love or stare at the fire. The lovely fire which is burning down, thundering away like the heart of a big animal in the grate. Then every now and then a burst of air like a burp as the lion digests the gazelle.

I had walked over to Bill and Betty's for dinner early as it was cold and I've run out of gas. The last of my classes ended and I came to a cold house. "There'll be a frost tonight," Bill said. I put my boots on the bricks of their hearth and we discussed which goddess Zeus was making love with when his wife Hera threw a net over them. Search as I may, I cannot find her name. Foolishly, I used it in a story for an anthology I am very keen to be included in. The deadline is overdue so I sent it off with a guess. Alcmene was the name I used. Tom at Megalong books sat on the floor and looked her up in a book while customers stepped patiently round him in the narrow passage. It wasn't Leda, so who else was it? And none of the other names of the loves of Zeus he read out rang a bell. So I took a punt on Alcmene.

I dreamt my brother died so I woke up panting, gasping, calling his name. I will ring Anne today and see if they are all alright. I seldom speak to him as he's out in his ute with a radio phone talking to other men at work. He rings at Christmas and when I go down to stay he takes me out to see the birds on his wetlands. But other than that I only see him rush past on his way to work while we drink tea in the kitchen. He is a man on fire. My mother said, "He'll be the richest man in the cemetery."

28th May, Tuesday. Mosman.

I watched Sophia Rose at her water lesson. It is a preparation for swimming called Water Babies, to strengthen them and to make them familiar with water. A new teacher arrived and the three babies, Emma, Henry and our girl were put through their paces. They were put under water and pulled along. Sophia does not yet know she needs to close her mouth so swallowed a lot of water.

They are dressed in tiny swimming costumes for these classes. Cathy bought a pink gingham costume the size of a hand for her brown-haired girl.

29th May, Wednesday. Mosman.

A yacht drags its wake like a silver train across the blue bay. A Norfolk Island pine sways in the breeze anchoring the land through the horizon, the sea, to the sky. The white datura lily droops outside Peri's bedroom window.

Justin is dancing in the hallway in high heels to the music coming from her father's study, a pop song with strong rhythm. She is dancing with an invisible partner. Every now and then she stops and walks in here to her mother's long mirror and moves her knees and feet to the beat, watching and correcting herself over and over. Then she goes back into the hall where she has rolled up the red kelim and dances to the staircase and back to the glass doors that open to the verandah which frame the sea, the Heads and Manly ferry. We don't speak. We are concentrating. I am watching her and she is watching herself trying for perfection. She maps a dance, I map her in her tiny black flared skirt, tall and twisting, turning and dancing like a beautiful pale solitary bird.

Peri is at her art class. She tore off this morning with a thermos and a bag of brushes and tubes of colour. "See you later!" she called as the dark green wooden gate slammed behind her. Many things she does nowadays interfere with her painting. It is like a secret lover to her. The sunroom has been turning into her studio. Piles of charcoal drawing cover the floor, a nude study is on the easel. A framed painting of Julie on the farm nursing a goose leans against a couch. The white painted piano has a painting leaning against it. She is a woman possessed. Happy, extended. Furious at how much she has to learn, excited and sometimes despairing, sometimes exhilarated. I have never seen Peri like this. Even when she was planting the orchard on the farm, she was not as deeply extended as now with painting. I hesitate to call her or to visit because I know I am one more thing that takes her from painting.

This morning Peri, before she left, asked me if I have read the *Poetics of Space* by Bachelard. "Well, yes and no. I read it but I can't remember it. In fact I remember reading a writer who dragged it round India with her and never read it but always meant to. That was Gabrielle Lord I remember now. She wrote that marvellous book *My Father's House*."

"Well," she said, "it's not a dragging around kind of book. There are dragging around books – Chatwin's books are good for that. But some books are like rocks – the only place to read them is alone and in your own bed.

"Now Rilke's books are not dragging around kind of books. You can read the same passage over and over again and one day you suddenly see it and it stays with you for life. Patrick White, you don't drag him around either.

"Harold Bloom takes real concentration. And it's so rich you've got to have concentrated reading and go over and over it because of its richness and density.

"Lechte's *Fifty Key Contemporary Thinkers* isn't for dragging around either. It intrigues me that book. I like to know about structuralism and so on."

I said, "Well, I've read Elizabeth Grosz on Julia Kristeva and Luce Irigaray and now I can't even remember the difference between them. And does it matter?"

"Well, I like a struggle and to know. If the language is just dense, I'll struggle with it. But if it's really obscure – and I know I'm not stupid – I think they want to keep their message a secret, so I give up. And when it's free floating like some of that new writing, it's got no anchor and you can get a bit lost in it. But I like people attempting new ways of writing and new ideas, and when it works it's wonderful. But a lot of the time it doesn't work. People like circularity. In your talk today for instance, you need to circle back to the beginning. That's what people like."

I said, "Well, I just like life. I don't need to find a circle. I am enchanted with what happens. That's my problem with some people. I just can't convince them that there isn't necessarily a point or a big theme to my new book. It just is about life. It's about a day; how a woman lives a day. Just what happens."

"Yes," she said, "You like a line, an ongoing line. That's what your writing is and that's a particular way of looking at the world. But the way I write, I like layers – layer upon layer. I know that's what I like. You are enchanted with just being. What you're not looking for in your writing is resolution and that's wise. We all know that this side of the grave there is no resolution. Life is a state of flux.

"But the writers I'm beholden to, they know themselves, the best and worst of themselves. They may be dreadful people, but they know the dark and are willing to go deeper. They're not just on the surface. I don't think you can be a great writer unless you have done the hard work and the self-analysis and you don't project it all out onto other people."

With that she finished making her bed, tossing the quilt over and smoothing it, arranging the tapestry cushions and walked from the room with me still trailing her as I had from the kitchen where she'd been stirring porridge when we first began talking.

Peri said, when I told her about taking Sophia with me when I had a facial before the book launch, "You are very good at caring for yourself. I am not bad at it, but you are better." This intrigued me, just as another statement did, made by a woman when I was signing a book. "I expected you to be more sophisticated." What did that mean? Over and over it turns like a piece of sand in that anxious oyster, my mind.

When I got home from giving the talk there were maps of Poland and Czechoslovakia on the kitchen table. Peri and Bob are going to the Tatra Mountains which they hadn't heard much of until this morning when they were recommended to them. Straight away they decided not to go to Spain. It sounds very gloomy to me, a setting for lieder in summer. Somebody is sitting on the hill singing a sad song about something lost. Very German. I wonder if this thread of dark green, a sort of mossy shaded longing, goes through everybody or if it's in those with German blood more particularly.

There is a story I made up to stop Sam being afraid of thunder. I got the last sentence from someone else.

> Once upon a time, we were all angels. The task of angels is to spin stories from threads of their gold and silver hair. And when angels have finished spinning enough thread for stories, they learn how to embroider the story into a myth. For this they need cruel needles which, especially when they are learning, prick their fingers and drops of blood fall. The sound of a drop of blood falling on the floor of heaven makes the sound of thunder. As soon as there is thunder, the oldest angel picks up his torch and looks for the drop of blood to mop it up with a brush of feathers from fallen angels. It is the light from this torch which makes the lightning. Sometimes, when the angel searching for the drop to mop is very old and feeble, it takes an inordinately long time to find so the lightning comes later than usual. But it always arrives. No angel ever misses finding the drop of blood from the prick of the needle and wiping it away, cleaning the floor of heaven. When a myth has been embroidered, it is given to a baby who is about to be born. This is the story of their life. It is their fate. It is folded within the child when it is born. The angel who embroidered the fate, and whose work it then is to watch over the child all its life, presses its finger to the lips of the child and says, 'Shhh don't tell them what you know'. And it is this mark of the angel's finger we all bear between our top lip and our nose.

30th May, Thursday. Mosman

Peri and I went to swim in Manly pool. I had no wish to go but the day was so sunny I went. People lay on the cement in the sun. An elderly stout man lying in shiny red bathers crossed his knees and looked up at the cloudless sky. Occasionally he rode an imaginary bike turning his feet round and round, then crossed his legs again and rested. The pool attendant took her lunch on a chair and then dozed in the sun, her face turning up like a sunflower. I got out of the pool and avoided a young blonde woman drying her hair in the sun, shaking it out letting the sun warm it. I walked round to the other side of the pool so such beauty couldn't see my flaws. It is easy to know when old that one was once beautiful. But it is hard when young to realise that the old were once beautiful.

31st May, Friday. Leura.

"My soul will triumph…" Graham Pushee is singing from Handel's opera *Alcina*. "Too right!" I mutter as I push my feet into my sandals and huddle off to make a cup of tea, pulling on my dressing gown in the cold. It is the last day of the autumn.

Sun is still pouring down, roses are blooming, two or three, not many but some. Yesterday I went to Monica's nursery and bought a tray of pink foxgloves, and a tray of apricot alyssum. Jeff has dug plots and with canterbury bells and some Phostrogen to put on them, I am keen to plant. But I have little faith there will be flowers. I do not entirely lack faith or else I would not plant at all. But I can never understand why others have such blooms and mine are so feeble. This is not false modesty. If the garden had worked or been better I wouldn't be modest. The trees are very successful. Sticks at the moment with some red leaves hanging like a few jewels in a ravished mansion, they will be beautiful in spring. I have seen it happen and have faith. The *Magnolia alba* is almost three metres high and covered in buds, one has burst like a white feather in the sun. I now know that it takes four years for a tree to put down roots and settle. Just as you have almost given up and think the tree is failing, it spreads branches and grows upwards. It is as if it had to put down roots properly and anchor itself well to give nourishment upwards.

I killed the dove tree with too much fertiliser. The leaves fell down around the trunk as if a woman stepped out of a ballgown. Again it sprouted, although it was out of season, but the effort killed it. You can love a thing or person too much. That is the lesson to learn over and over. If you love a child too much it may be that you will never be able to fill them. It is as if you have created an emptiness, an unfillable well.

Every day I struggle to write a book I can neither abandon nor finish in the way I hoped. I fear this may be obvious. I did not know events would happen that I could not tell with ardour, but reluctantly and with shame. I meant to write a happy book, something to give courage. However, I want to know how it ends.

June

1st June, Saturday. Leura.

The first day of winter. A second bloom has burst on the magnolia. This one blushed with pink as if it tore. An eerie beautiful full moon poured through the black pines. A dingo's gold and silver eye among grey furred clouds. I almost howled back at it. Olive bread toasted and with ricotta cheese spread on and raspberry jam is very good. I had it for dinner while that dingo watched hungrily outside the window. I threw crusts out and do not expect to find any tomorrow.

2nd June, Sunday. Leura.

My neighbours Betty and Bill drove round the corner as I turned to leave their front door. We sat warming our feet by their fire speaking of their planned cruise up the coast of Norway and its fjords. They are going to tour some medieval shrines in Spain after a cruise of the Orkney islands. We looked at maps.

King parrots, the males with scarlet heads and all with emerald bodies, ate sunflower seed from a plate hanging outside the window. I remarked that there had been flocks of tiny green silver eyes in the birches in my garden. Betty took down a bird book and reported that they were hunting insects and travel in flocks from Tasmania. They have been banded and found to return to some gardens year after year. They fly overnight. We wondered if they do this to navigate by the stars or to escape hawks. But then owls could prey on them. Betty said, "You know, an owl will run its wing along a hedge to scare out small animals and then Boom! It pounces!"

Then, as it was after noon, they brought out bread, cheese and fruit for lunch. We sat watching the parrots eating level with our eyes. Two young were there, females with black beaks and green heads. "Oh look Odile!" I said to their six-year-old granddaughter who had joined us, "One is eating with her mother." "No it's not," Betty said, "that's a male," the bird having the scarlet head. Odile told me a dazzling tale of her young sister falling asleep in the bathroom hand basin and turning the cold water on, sleeping as it ran over her legs.

Last Friday a haircut. Very short. The cutter's name is Possum. Her long hair in a French roll, is tightly coiled and made into a little nest on her crown. She wears an apron, has perfect pale skin and auburn hair. We seldom speak. I am always in a bad mood slumped in a chair at the hairdresser's and never wish to discuss anything but the cut and that as briefly as possible. Possum knows this although I have not said so. She leaves me in peace and gives me a long-snipping-short-cut of great finesse and detail. I walk out ten years younger.

Now because of the cut and the cold day, a cold neck, so the new scarlet scarf. No sun all day, only silver light falls through the tall dark gum trees. I want several people to love me. Family, friends and lover. Do they? Maybe. Perhaps. Does it matter? We cannot live well without love. I have love. I know it. Why do I want more? Unsatisfied desire. And as for that old dog love, the one named lover, I live seldom seeing him, speaking on the telephone. Letters sometimes pass between us; otherwise, silence and space. Silence and space are things I love. But today I would like to see him.

Red mushrooms with white spots have come up in gardens and on paths. Peri could hardly believe her eyes last weekend when she saw them. They are the kind illustrated in children's books. I had thought they were just an artist's invention for fairies to sit on.

But here they are, each year. And the big lush gold-topped ones are crumbling away. A few traditional mushrooms, edible, have come up in the lawn. Something so fragile cracks concrete.

Eggplant is at its best now and Jerusalem artichokes are still in the shops. Pears and apples are piled up and plums have gone before the chutney was made. Cathy's recipe for a Thai way of cooking eggplant and bean curd is good. The palm sugar makes a difference and is easy to buy now:

> vegetable oil
> 250 grams firm bean curd, drained and wiped dry
> 2 red chillies, chopped and seeds removed
> 2 cloves of garlic, finely chopped
> 1 shallot, chopped
> 250 grams slender eggplants, thinly chopped
> 1 tsp palm sugar
> 4 tbsp lime juice
> 1 tbsp fish sauce
> half a cup of basil leaves.
> dash of oyster sauce

Shallow fry the bean curd in oil until lightly coloured on both sides. Drain and set aside.

Heat 1 tbsp oil in a wok and fry the combined chillies, garlic and shallot. Add eggplant and cook until it softens. Move this to one side in the wok. If you need more than 1 tbsp oil, remember the eggplant absorbs the oil so add more if you wish.

Add the palm sugar, lime juice, fish sauce and bean curd and simmer about 2–3 minutes with the wok lid on, to allow the flavours to develop and be absorbed into the bean curd and also to stop evaporation.

Now toss in the torn basil and mix. Serve with jasmine rice or noodles.

3rd June, Monday. Leura.

Day is done. There's silence. I have been going over the difficulties of being a mother. I have always despised people who talked about this as if it were a great sacrifice and somehow a virtue. But now I admit that thinking over and over what I might have done differently, while not really a help, makes me see I can change nothing from the past. But I can approach my daughter with openness and trust. Just to keep going, trying to rebuild the friendship.

There was a beautiful blonde woman who came to my classes last month who wrote an honest story about how she longed for a stable love affair. She told how each time she went out to meet a man she had to gather the courage to tell her daughters she wouldn't be home that evening. Then she faced their reproaches. I couldn't say to her that she was turning her back on evenings she would later perhaps regret not spending at home. But all that is too pious and irrelevant when you are young and desperately searching for a lover. There seems no way to say the search is somehow a hopeless one in most cases, that the very need that rules it seems, in its desperation, to destroy the possibility of a decent relationship. But I can hardly tell a woman to stay home. I went out. I went out a lot.

And is that the reason now I have this difficulty with my daughter? Maybe it is. Maybe it has nothing to do with it. I go over this wondering what to do next. There's a core of sadness that can't be cured except by being accepted by my own child. And I don't know if she ever will.

The really queer thing about it is, I thought we had a wonderful relationship and that she thought I was as splendid as I thought she was. It's a shock to find out what your child thinks of you. So I keep ringing up leaving messages about once a week and hoping that time may soften her.

Now I think I must just live here and not think about her and not rob the day of its richness. Each time I start to think about my daughter and how to bring about forgiveness I lose my grip. So on the whole I put the whole matter from me, set it aside and hope it will improve. But I'm tired of waiting. Yet I must give her time. How long have we? That's what I wonder at times.

Today six punnets of the apricot alyssum went in. As I straightened up, the first stars were coming out. It was cool. I came inside.

In my letter box, Jean Perry left a page that Dr Claire sent her after the lunch when we discussed ageing last week. Jean said, "This is what I think is probably important to consider on ageing." It is supposed to be a 17th Century Nun's Prayer.

> *LORD Thou knowest better than I know myself that I am growing older and will someday be old. Keep me from the fatal habit of thinking I must say something on every subject and on every occasion. Release me from striving to straighten out everybody's affairs. Make me thoughtful but not moody: helpful but not bossy. With my vast store of wisdom, it seems a pity not to use it all, but thou knowest Lord that I want few friends at the end.*
>
> *Keep my mind free from the recital of endless details; give me wings to get the point. Seal my lips on my aches and pains. They are increasing, and the love of rehearsing them is becoming sweeter as the years go by. I dare not ask for grace enough to enjoy the tales of other's pains, but help me to endure them with patience.*
>
> *I dare not ask for improved memory, but for a growing humility and a lessening cocksureness when my memory seems to clash with the memories of others. Teach me the glorious lesson that occasionally I may be mistaken.*
>
> *Keep me reasonably sweet; I do not want to be a saint – some of them are hard to live with – but a sour old person is one of the crowning works of the devil. Give me the ability to see good things in unexpected places and talents in unexpected people. And, give me, O Lord, the grace to tell them so.* AMEN

5th June, Wednesday. Leura.

My right boot's full of water. I've been digging up hellebores from Phyllis's garden two houses away. I filled a wheelbarrow just digging some from a path around old azaleas under maples. Phyllis taught me, years ago, to put lupins in pots and dig them in under trees to keep their roots safe from the tree. Her husband has died since I came to live here but she mows her big lawn and gardens in her navy straw hat, year in year out. She told me to help myself to the hellebores, which cost about $20 each in shops. They are called Christmas roses as the story goes that the child who had no gift for Christ wept when the Wise Men bought their gifts and from the tears grew this flower.

Yesterday Jeff dug up five rhododendrons. We put them in the front garden and also in a newly dug bed. I was so excited I couldn't sleep. And got up and peered out of the back glass doors in the starlight trying to see. No success. So I went out at first light looking at the plants in their new beds. Nan tells me they will go into shock. These are eight-year-old shrubs, so are big, and in the first week cannot take up much moisture or food therefore must be watered daily, "Keep the water up to them, darling, or they'll die." Mats of roots surround almost everything under the pines. Jeff rolled up one of these mats and took it away. All the alyssum and foxgloves and canterbury bells and white primula are planted. We tore at the work like sinners. It took five pots of tea and half a chocolate cake to keep us going. I forgot everything else. The world fell away like water in the hands. It felt pure, almost holy. The man looked wrecked. His ponytail drenched in sweat and the misty rain that fell for a while. He dug hole after hole. Two big azaleas were moved also. And three roses. *Virgo* was under a pine and long and thin like an anorexic. Now the long white buds should come in summer, along with the other roses in the back bed, which is airy and in full sun when it comes. The sun poured down today. People held out their hands in the street and looked up at the sky revelling in such a day.

A letter today from a farmer at Tumby Bay where I was born, inviting me to come and stay. She has a big red Honda 4-wheel motor bike and a red kelpie and says "We do a lot of sheep droving." She's 70 and I'm tempted. But I probably won't go as the writer almost always disappoints. Like the garden, these realities are best left to exist in the reader's imagination. Few can live up to themselves. And not all that many gardens can either.

For example, a famous local land agent walking down the street said to her client, on passing my house, that it was mine. The client remarked she'd read my work and Annie, looking over the fence, gesturing at the garden said, "Yes, it just shows what a good writer Kate is." I treasure this remark because it shows so well how disappointing facts can be. It is not that I lied, it is just that every plant exists in perfection in some reader's imagination. Not everything has flourished, some I've poisoned and some let die for want of water. Some just died for their own reasons never fathomed. Some went mad and killed off other plants. I lost as much as I planted. Most things went in the wrong places. Many plants have been moved three times. It is easy to plant a garden but hard to maintain it, I'll say that.

I would not now take Edna Walling's advice on the matter of daffodils in lawns. They look pretty for a month and woeful after that. When all about are mowing theirs, you must let your lawn lapse long and unkempt while the bulbs die off and build up carbohydrate for next year's blooms. This takes about two months and is maddening if you like anything neat. I don't particularly, but I can see clearly all around me good green grass, velvety and smooth, and my own shambles. I always have big bunches of daffodils for Caro's birthday on the 5th of September.

If I get any money from any place in the next week or so I will buy left-over bulbs cheaply and put them in.

The garden has put aside my anxiety about who thinks what of me in a most particular way. Standing there sodden, by the laden barrow, I did not care. No, I was exhilarated, almost ecstatic. The hellebores lay there like ferns from a forest, so many I do not know where to put them. The woman, the barrow, the green plants, the evening star appearing. It could have been Eden without Adam.

8th June, Saturday. Leura.

Hugh and Cathy are here for the Queen's Birthday long weekend. They brought Sophia and Sam came too. I lay sleeping with the two children last night listening to them breathe. A feeling of serenity and happiness came over me. Sam ground his teeth from time to time, sleeping beside me. Sophia purred on, breaking wind very sweetly, the result of her new diet of vegetables. I lay with such an accomplishment of serenity pouring over me, I knew joy. I saw one doesn't need to sleep much when surrounded by deep pleasure.

Woolfie, my old friend who came with her husband Gordon to live with me when I first bought this house, came up. She stayed at Varuna to begin a new book. Gordon brought up their nine-year-old daughter Kitty, who ran round the big garden at Varuna. Peter the director served champagne and almond meal chocolate cake for afternoon tea and we sold books. Woolfie has written a book about motherhood and mathematics called *Leaning Towards Infinity* and it's short-listed for all the big prizes.

13th June, Thursday. Canberra.

A white gum has the morning light hitting its trunk outside this bedroom window. Patricia and I loll around drinking tea, talking about yesterday. She drove four hours to Bowral and back for lunch at Peppers resort where I gave a talk organised by Shearer's Bookshop. It was a freezing day.

Patricia made beetroot and potato soup for dinner to have with the sourdough bread I bought from Warwick's bakery. This is how to make the soup:

Patricia's Beetroot and Potato Soup

Boil 1 or 2 bunches of beetroot with the tops removed. When tender if pricked with a fork, cool and slip the peel off. Chop and put into a blender.

Boil half as many potatoes and do the same.

Fry 2 or 3 onions in olive oil with 3 or 4 cloves of garlic.

Blend all these vegetables with beef stock, which in this case came from a carton of real beef stock. You can make your own if you have time.

When all is blended, pour into a pan and heat. Add some chopped beetroot leaves. Boil for 5 minutes or so until the leaves are tender. The leaves can be bitter so use no more than a cup or two.

Serve with salt and pepper and a bowl of yogurt or sour cream and bread.

Patricia later told me she puts a tablespoon of white wine vinegar in all vegetable soups and never uses cream in soup.

15th June, Saturday. Canberra.

Last night Patricia gave a dinner and sold a painting. So when I said goodbye to her to come here to Marion and Cosmo's house, we were happy. We slapped each other on the back, kissed and hugged. Life is good, life is short. Life with friends is best of all.

Marion walked in to the breakfast table from the garden with her arms full of newspapers. I said idly, as we both have books out waiting for review, "And what trouncings have we had today?" I was soon to know. "You've got a review here," she said reading on. After a while she passed the paper over. An ex-South African journalist had gone to town on my book.

To write about South Africa and not offend people, even though you hold your pen on a thousand horrors, can be regarded simply as Mission Impossible. Last week I had a letter from a Ugandan man, James Bakeime in Kampala, who operates Nile Safaris. He acknowledged the book's arrival and said "When I was reading about your experience in South Africa it is as though you had read my mind (especially when you talked about Jo'burg)." Ah but then James is black you see.

In Johannesburg visitors will one day be able to report what they actually saw and felt. As it was, I did not report on all that I saw. I censored myself beyond belief.

17th June, Monday. Leura.

Yesterday Marion and Cosmo drove me to the train station at lunch time and went off to a nearby market. I boarded the train and read that brilliant whodunit *Snow Falling on Cedars* by David Gutterson, then slept among the ashes of my chagrin. Seven hours later I walked into the freezing house wreathed in fog. Dinner in an overcoat looks like a wartime newsreel.

All the transplanted big rhododendrons have survived so far. I ran out in the starlight and put the hose on the largest. It is not a thing to be recommended, digging up these big shrubs when about to flower, especially not in a warmer climate, but it seems that here it can be done. Flowers will come in Spring.

When I got in from Canberra, under my door was a copy of a poem by the great religious poet George Herbert.

> *Love bade me welcome: yet my soul drew back,*
> *Guiltie of dust and sinne.*
> *But quick-ey'd Love, observing me grow slack*
> *From my first entrance in,*
> *Drew nearer to me, sweetly questioning,*
> *If I lack'd any thing.*
>
> *A guest, I answer'd, worthy to be here:*
> *Love said, You shall be he.*
> *I the unkinde, ungratefull? Ah my deare,*
> *I cannot look on thee.*
> *Love took my hand, and smiling did reply,*
> *Who made the eyes but I?*
>
> *Truth, Lord, but I have marr'd them: let my shame*
> *Go where it doth deserve.*
> *And know you not, sayes Love, who bore the blame?*
> *My deare, then I will serve.*
> *You must sit down, sayes Love, and taste my meat:*
> *So I did sit and eat.*

18th June, Tuesday. Leura.

The wood has not come. Once the woodman came and said he had once read a book. We both impressed each other the woodman and I. It seemed such an original thing to say dropping off the load of iron-bark at the gates. For the first time in my life I do not feel strong enough to bring in a load of wood under the house in the barrow without help. Sam usually helps me. He is so strong and loves to work. He sits having morning tea on a pile of wood, finishes the food and drink and stands up, pulls on his gloves and begins again. Hugh was shocked when I told him Sam had brought in two and a half cubic metres in a day. He said I should not let him work like that. But he loves to do it. To work with a child is beautiful. They say the most original things.

There's a box of chestnuts I raked under the house waiting for Sam to come up and have a stall to sell them on the footpath as he did last year.

In Canberra a man was selling roasted chestnuts in the street. He reminded me of the chestnut seller in *La Bohéme*. I've seen a set designer's sketch of that above a bed somewhere. Buying some I asked what he did the rest of the year. He said he gathered native seeds for a living. He said, "I live in the bush." He seemed like a pixie, and had a brown Tyrolean hat and maybe a jerkin to match. At Marion's we ate the chestnuts sitting at the table drinking wine. They were delicious and go well, she said, in chicken stew. In return, I was given Jerusalem artichokes to bring home. They are cooking now to make scallop and Jerusalem artichoke soup. This is how it's done:

315 grams Jerusalem artichokes
1 onion
1 medium potato
600 ml chicken stock
200 grams scallops
100 ml fresh cream
1 egg yolk
chopped parsley
pepper and salt

Boil the artichokes for 10 minutes, then put them under a cold tap and scrub off the skin. Slice onion and fry in butter. Peel and slice the potato and fry it with onion and artichokes. Stir until they are covered with butter or they will blacken. Add half the chicken stock. Cook covered for 10 minutes. Blend or mash this mixture. Reheat.

Separate the scallops, keeping the coral whole. Then chop the white. Mix the cream and egg yolk and add remaining stock to this. Pour into the pan. Reheat soup gently but do not let it boil. Just before serving add scallops and then remove from heat. Add parsley, salt and pepper.

19th June, Wednesday. Leura.

High pale pink torn clouds were gliding fast over an ice blue sky early this morning. I should not be here. The wood has come. Dumped across the drive ready to trip a walker.

Woolfie's book is here. I bought it with the Public Lending Right money that came. Last night I lay and read. When George our friend spoke to her about mathematics years ago while Woolfie held her baby, he didn't know this book would be the outcome and I guess neither did she. And now to the wood.

Later

The postman came by on his motorbike.

"Doing your bit for the environment I see," he said.

"Well I do worry about where this comes from," I said.

"Miles and miles away. A million ring-barked trees. I am growing my own wood now. A certified vermin, tree lucerne," he said nodding to the wood heap at the gate.

"What's that?"

"It's that tree over there." He pointed to a waving tree with white blossom across the road by the new drystone wall fence. It looked like a broom or white wattle to me.

"Yes, I forget it's botanical name, starts with C... It cuts up in small pieces well. Did you know Melbourne is burning a million and a half cubic metres of wood a year now? And I suppose we'll only stop when it gets like Russia, with the inside of the window covered in ice because they've burnt all their fuel. People ought to be able to go out and see nature at their door, not have to come up here to see it. I wrote a poem, as a matter of fact, the other day. But I can't remember what I wrote."

"I have that trouble myself."

I stood at the gate by the barrow listening to Steve in his yellow helmet and raincoat warming to his topics.

"I've planted a lot of eucalyptus but it dies now. Funny isn't it, our natives are dying, but our pernicious poisonous weeds grow. Still, I reckon there's room for us all. People are real fascists about plants. They run a plant apartheid. Some of them hate cotoneaster you know. After all some of us are fascists about people and we once had the country run like that. We killed off the local people because we thought of them as weeds. I reckon there's room for all of us."

With this he revved up the bike and drove off down the path, a happy man.

When the wood was in I hosed down the path and came inside. Patricia's beetroot soup, with a head of fennel among big beef bones, was boiling. After it was pureed I took a bowl over to Nan. Jude was there in the drive not going in because of the steps and her wheelchair. Her partner Tom Folwell had rung from his exhibition in Noumea to say it was an enormous success. Jude said, "I've been crying all day." This artist works here in extreme isolation, and some say he's a genius. He is hardly known here. Yet the French in Noumea have gone wild.

Bill stopped his car as I walked home yesterday from Katoomba and gave me a lift. The force of the work he'd done was with him in the car; it could be felt.

"I've been cleaning out a lady's gutters. Do you know they were sprouting!"

I said, "That reminds me of something I've just read in the Bible about harvesting grain on the roof. Do you know it?"

He said he didn't, though he's a scholar and reads till midnight. We spoke a while about the George Herbert poem he'd left me and about an article which said that Christ had made 'a bridge of bread' in saying "Take, eat, do this in remembrance of me."

"What a lovely, lovely image Kate. The minds of some people! What a wonderful way to think, a bridge of bread! So even if the disciples forgot, we would remember. Amazing!" And with that, he drew up and I got out.

Now *Sheep shall safely graze* is being sung by Gillian Fisher with the King's Consort. More and more it's clear that quiet days at Leura make me happy. Such a day it's been. The pleasure of the wood, the luxury of it. The postman, the news of Tom's success. Currawongs eating pickled eggs thrown in the garden after Suzie cleaned the fridge. They love potatoes and eggs. A wattle bird flew in and perched swaying on the bough of the apple outside the kitchen window as I stood blending the beetroot. It reminded me that when I first came I watched sparrows pecking at the soft buds and did not know what kind of tree it was.

It is my mother's hand which writes this. After a day's work, her wrists were like this. I put out my hand to settle a towel by the fire and was startled, as if it was her hand that lifted the towel. Our parents inhabit us.

Gold things all day. A tall gold streaming star last night when I went to bring in logs. It hung like a golden tear on the sky's face. There above, heaving across the arch of the Milky Way, Hera's breast milk.

Today, passing a garden a man I couldn't see called to another "Anne's got a daffodil out!" I thought it must be a jonquil as it is too early here surely. Yet round the corner of Nan's garden later I saw a clump of daffodils trembling in the breeze. And there was something else. The yellow quinces glowing there in the blue dish as I turned my head to think. But it wasn't them, and it wasn't the first yellow poppy bursting from a pot of poppies. Neither was it the brazen gold lemon I picked, the last on the tree. On which I fling the golden rain of the night's harvest every morning. I don't know what it was, but whatever it was, it was golden, that much I know.

20th June, Thursday. Leura.
Reading Horace on ageing – James Michie's translation in Penguin Classics:

Don't ask, we may not know, Leucouno
What the gods plan for you or me.
Leave the Chaldees to parse
The sentence of the stars.

Better to beat the outcome, good or bad,
Whether Jove purposes to add,
Fresh windows to the past
Or to make this the last

Which now tires out the Tuscan sea and mocks
Its strength with barricades of rocks,
Be wise, strain clear the wine
and prune the rambling vine

Of expectation. Life's short. Even while
We talk Time, hateful, runs a mile.
Don't trust tomorrow's bough
For fruit. Pluck this, here now."

I've remembered the other golden thing. It was the postman at the gate. A bee, in his yellow coat and hat with big black boots, his black glasses never raised, bringing me that honey, letters from the world's hive.

21st June, Friday. Leura.

Athena, the patron Goddess of Athens, whose symbol is the owl, chose for the supreme gift for mankind, not gold nor jewels but the olive tree, from whose fruit 'an extraordinary liquid could flow to serve as food for Mankind, to alleviate his wounds, strengthen his body and lighten his night.' I have been wondering yet again, having found this in a book left here, if an olive would grow here against the north-facing wall.

"Give up on fruit, plant a nut," Peri said with her usual asperity listening to my plan years ago.

I didn't take her advice. Lately though, it's become clear that both fruit and nuts are what I ought to plant. Jude's and Tom's great chestnut yields barrow loads of nuts. It may be, and perhaps

Steve the postman has had an effect, that whoever lives here after me could be glad to have pears, more apples, a persimmon, an olive. (Olives grow in Greece in tough climates like this.) We are inclined to shrink from planting what grows well in colder places.

There have been less than a dozen cherries from the two trees I planted years ago, but this may improve if the birds can be kept off. The apples, the same. Which reminds me, today in the mail Steve sent his poem that he couldn't remember:

> *Little polly parrots*
> *sitting in a row*
> *transforming into a rainbow*
> *as feathers flutter*
> *green red, blue and yellow*
> *accepting their lot*
> *exploding under No. 4 shot!*

With this came a note continuing a second conversation we had yesterday in the street. Steve had said, "I've got a theory of how to clean up the Murray without all that expense. The PhDs haven't thought of it. I might sound a nut, but I have developed this theory from my own observations." Now he writes:

> As a result of your 'wood heap' I thought of a simple way to fix the Murray River based on personal observation of Eastern Creek which I fished as a boy. The water was clear but full of carp but not overly so. The Murray is cloudy and full of carp. The difference is the effect of Casuarinas on the river banks. So plant them along the Murray and predators of carp should develop – cormorants, kingfishers, snakes, terrapins, to name a few.
>
> > *Hello Sun!*
> > *Lighten my heart.*
> > *Hello Moon!*
> > *Take my hand and*
> > *Lead me through the dark.*
>
> A pagan thought I had during a bout of abject loneliness,
> Regards, Stephen.

A letter today from Woolfie inviting me, as she puts it, to come for a float in their boat. Her book kept me up half the night. She writes that she'd like me to explain the world to her. This makes me laugh. Neither of us have ever wavered in knowing what we wanted from the world. But I don't know if we have ever understood what the world wants from us or, more particularly, how it works. Does anybody know? We only know what we believe.

How can anybody explain anything to anybody about how the world works. I watch Peri, who has a view that simply leaves me agape. She plans ten years or more ahead. Her grandchildren's careers are even thought of, not at all directed, but plans are set in place that will ensure they can have what they might need if a certain career is their desire. My plans, while not exactly without ambition, are daily bound up with writing something and making sure that there is a room tidy enough into which I could bring a policeman if one called.

When I spoke of this to Phil he laughed and said, "What are you expecting the police for?"

I said, "Two called once when a dog bit me. One asked if I wanted it shot."

I do not know where these habits come from. Some of them, like this one, are so ingrained one is not even aware of them. Like Banraku puppeteers, they creep behind us ruling our days while we romp on believing we are acting of our own free will.

Ghilly and I had a long talk yesterday on the telephone. She is rehearsing for *Lucia di Lammermoor*. We discussed criticism and how to accept it and learn from it.

Years ago I met a critic buying stockings. For some reason I can't recall, although we'd never met, I recognised her and asked if she was so-and-so who'd given a book of mine a rave review. She said indeed she was. She said I should be careful. I had done what others dream of doing, and doing that engenders jealousy at times. She herself had once had a houseboat. She said "You can have no idea how much rage and envy that engendered. It is very dangerous to live a dream that others dream." I can't see that happening on this occasion.

Once I offended Woolfie. I laughed at structuralism and she didn't speak to me for three years. I was puzzled for a long time, then wore away and gave up. Then ages later she explained what I'd done.

When I told her somebody simply could not believe we could fall out over such a thing, she laughed and said "Kate! I've just seen a wonderful play in London called *Art*. It's about two friends who fall out because one of them bought a painting and the other couldn't understand why! I liked the play so much I've bought the script!"

Now time, I suppose, has poured oil on troubled waters. Which brings me to olive oil on chicken over an open fire. Because the fire goes night and day it's pleasant to boil the kettle, grill meat, boil a dish of whole apples in sago or in brown rice with sugar on the stove top, or make lentil and ham bone soup. It gives a primitive feeling.

The recipe, if that is the word – method might be more apt – is to cut a chicken in half, rub it with Dijon mustard and then pour olive oil over it. Leave it an hour or so or overnight. In a grilling wire, place the two sides, skin side down over a fire. After fifteen minutes or so, depending on the heat of the fire, turn and cook the other side. Serve this with boiled potatoes or mashed potatoes or rice – things which mop up the juices – and green salad. For this it is not necessary to use extra virgin olive oil as so much of it burns in the fire.

And because today Tom is having a party on coming home from Noumea, I'm making a kind of humus. This is made by sprouting chick peas in a bowl in a cupboard for four or five days. To do this soak them covered in water for several hours. Top up with more water until they have soaked well. Drain and leave in the dark – no need to spread them out, they will sprout anyway. Rinse off daily and return to cupboard. When they have sprouted, blend them with olive oil, rock salt and several cloves of garlic in an electric blender. Dried tomatoes and their oil can be added in the blender, or sweet chilli sauce.

This is a stalwart dish, full of good things, enzymes and so forth, good for colds and for cold weather sandwiches. Serve with chopped Italian parsley and bread. It will keep in the refrigerator for a week or so if covered. A lidded jar is best.

23rd June, Sunday. Leura.

Stormy weather. Rain and wind. A chill on the neck from a draught at this window. The fire sulks and slumps out. Again it's lit. Again, it dies. Perhaps the chimney needs cleaning. In ten years it's not been done. Suzie's husband cleans chimneys.

Hugh and Cathy are coming up for a holiday so I've been washing blankets. Draped around the room they reminded me of the bleaching of sheets which my mother did because the quality was better when bleached at home. Cheaper too. My father, when first married, came home to find the garden draped and called in surprise, "Why are you making tents Tommy?" She told this tale laughing because it showed in what a genteel way he'd been brought up with a mother who did not bleach her own sheets.

"Jelly for birthdays!" my mother would say scornfully to indicate our grandmother did not know how to cook, or how to celebrate.

My mother's meals were lavish, cream on baked custard made with a dozen eggs. Irish stew thickened with milk, flour and parsley sauce, a queer addition but good, making it more of a fricassee. Cream poured over boiled cauliflower as a sauce. A fresh sponge made daily while my parents washed up. The Mixmaster would be beating, the fire built up to heat the oven for the sponge. By eleven, the sponge would be on the table, two sealed together with her own apricot jam and whipped vanilla cream, then covered in the cream. It is possible to learn to hate sponge.

Beneath the cedar tree my parents sat having morning tea with the farm workmen. There is a photograph of them under this tree in the days of their greatest hardship, when fighting to keep their farm. My mother has just taken a bite of sponge. His hat with holes in the crown is on his head. This is the hat he used to take off, blow smoke from his pipe into, put on his head and make his sons roar and bend over with laughter. My mother at the kitchen window watching would say, "Come and look at Brink and the boys. You are so lucky to have a father like this." Electra stood beside Clytemnestra, yearning, watching from the sink.

24th June, Monday. Leura.

Wind rattles the windows, the treetops, the fire roars. I laughed when I walked out this morning, the fire so stoked it had made the rooms almost tropical. Fed up with my parsimonious guilty frugality with wood, I'd heaped the fire with logs last night. Now I see, reading Reay Tannahill's *Food in History*, that Greece had the same problem of deforestation with the surge of population when trees were felled to make way for cultivation.

Later

I have been out planting roses. *Carmina, Fantin Latour, Brandy, Gloire Dijon*, and a dozen mixed daffodils around them. Looking up the list of roses I planted in 1987 there are 74 listed. But where are they? I can't believe it. I stared at the list, pages of it written by hand. The names are familiar mostly, but some I feel I've never heard of, let alone bought and planted. But I remember the day when Philippa and I drove back from Honeysuckle Cottage at Mt Bold laden with roses, and the car broke down. We were towed with Philippa steering the car. We rang Gordon and Woolfie, who were here at this house. Gordon came with baby Kitty in the back so there wasn't enough room for all the roses. We left them in the car at the service station and next day a librarian from Canberra helped me to plant them. But where did they go? I go over and over it.

29th June, Saturday. Elanora, Queensland.

Under the mango tree Sam is beside me washing golf balls we found in the orchard beside the golf course. Julie and Anton, the caretakers on this, Peri's farm, are varnishing the verandah. I came in for lunch after gathering golf balls, feeding geese, ducks, bantams and watching Sam climb a Morton Bay fig tree, to find it was only ten thirty.

We flew here yesterday for the school holidays. Over the swathe of coast, the green water shining, the strange mountains following the white coast, erratic as a sick pulse, we flew north. Suddenly palm trees, bougainvillea, surfers in the water, we landed with a thump. Coolangatta. Julie met us and drove us to the farm. Allergic to the grass I've got asthma.

An ibis stalked through the orchard and a blue wren jerked about on the lawn as I went down to check on Sam who is selling golf balls at the gate.

At least there are no cats here. Julie is now catching rats with traps. Before this no creature was ever killed by anybody except Anton and myself. Anton shoots crows which take eggs from geese and other poultry sitting on eggs. They swoop down when the bird gets up for food and water. I kill roosters when there are more than needed for fertile eggs. But no trap has ever been set or gun shot even for foxes though there have been raids that left Julie weeping. Dead and dying poultry lying around a pen of blood and feathers. After the last raid, when the fox slithered in under a gate which has since been blocked, Julie found a six-week-old duckling she had reared with half a dozen others, still alive but paralysed. She took it home and massaged its legs which she said were cold and became warm after a few days. It began to walk in a splayed leg way, awkward but moving. Bringing it out to the farm daily to mix with the other ducklings from the brood meant it was pecked and harassed until she put it into the dam. It could not really swim but sprayed around desperately. Yet the next day it could swim more or less normally.

30th June, Sunday. Elanora.

The sun pours down like lava on the neck. Earlier Sam was slashing the trees with some bamboo he'd whittled so I had to explain that it damages the tree. Now he is picking oranges. The fruit is so juicy it runs out in small torrents as we eat spitting seeds on the grass. Card tricks are his passion; it goes with being seven. So every hour or so he brings out the pack and asks me to chose a card. "Oh darn," he says as he can't show the same one back as he is supposed to. Riddles, magic, juggling, are his obsession. Standing talking to the twin goats, their noses nuzzling him as he strokes their horns, flinging grain around with it falling over the heads of the honking geese, these are the things that please him. And it pleases me to watch.

July

2nd July, Tuesday. Elanora.

Crows fly like ink blots against the air letter sky. Calling their melancholy cry which reminds me of the yellow wheat fields where we took our children for beach holidays. Perhaps it was the sad cry of marriage. Endless, remorseless, unsalvageable.

    The young willow by the dam was trembling. I looked and saw a goat eating bark. It had climbed round the fence which Julie had built and taken out into the waters edge. Peri will be upset because she has treasured this tree, hoarding it when others died. But you can have goats or you can have trees, you can't have both. I remind myself that this is play, this is a holiday farm. Generations of children have come here, ridden their horses, fed the geese, watched the peacocks display and so on. Some have cried all the way home on the plane, Peri says. I feel upset when I see the damage the pretty goats are doing when a sheep would have eaten the grass in the goose pen and so stopped them nesting there where the crows can eat the eggs, which is what the goats are meant to do.

    Julie is an animal lover of Franciscan proportions. There are many stories of her devotion. There is no creature she does not love, except crows and snakes.

    Last night Sam and I blocked off the roosting pen so that today we could catch a bantam rooster and the drakes. However, when we entered with the fish net there were only three hens left. We'd not seen a hole in our barricade. So tonight it will be walled tightly. A white peacock stalking past calls it's raucous cry; an angel with devil's song.

Sam and I are reading *Grimm's Fairy Tales*. He begins at the top of the page regardless of the fact it is half way though a sentence. That was where he ceased last night, so that is where he begins next day.

Peri's granddaughter Natali is due to arrive in the next hour. I am hoping she will play some cards and board games with Sam. Her mother Sheridan says Natali is making an end of the year ball gown for her design class and her brother brought four friends over and one slept on it on the couch where she'd spread it. She gave him a black eye.

3rd July, Wednesday. Elanora.

Pale grey brolgas on pink legs stalked around like umbrellas. Sam and I went to the Currumbin Bird Sanctuary. "Will the birds sing if we push a button?" he asked, thinking it a museum. Koalas sat in the forks of trees sleeping and some blinking, searching around as if looking for a ship out at sea. Two men were dragging fresh branches of gum leaves to replenish tin vases lashed to the trunks of the trees in which the koalas sat. I was very taken with this place thinking, before we went, it was somewhere that bird feeding on a grand scale went on and that was all. But lorikeets by the thousand, gold and red, are fed at ten and four. We saw none of that. Just a great snake being picked up by its tail by a keeper, winding round like a tightly wound spring, curling up on itself to the keeper's shoulder. He quickly removed it from near his neck as its method of killing prey is by strangling.

Speaking of strangling, killing two roosters and a drake this morning, I accidentally strangled one of the roosters in the net. Suddenly it seemed very quiet; they are screeching, wild birds, fighting and energetic.

Sheridan, Natali's mother who arrived last night, seeing the platter of dressed poultry on the table, said, "We are going to do a story about this, the ethics of it. Mind you, I agree with you, it's dishonest to eat what you scorn others for killing."

Natali said "Yes, call it The Killer, The Cook and the Chook."

Then, taking her camera she photographed us under the mango with the dish of dressed poultry, a branch of oranges, pecans, celery and dried figs as it is with these the duck is to be stuffed.

"You are the only person who has come to the farm and who kills anything," Sheridan said, neither judging nor praising.

4th July, Thursday. Elanora.

Someone is standing in a boat fishing in the river, Sam is cracking pecans with a brass crocodile, Julie is mowing lawns and Natali is lying on her stomach in the sun studying. I have been chasing three drakes with a net on a handle as Julie says there is no need for three, for only two ducks. They swam off while I stood on the bank with Sam, stymied for the moment. I have been wanting to try a James Beard recipe for pheasant or guinea fowl and now I think I will use a drake with a few adjustments.

The neighbour's three dogs howled half the night. Crows called at dawn. There are too many crows but now Anton has no gun and can't borrow one. Julie has been setting a crow trap with the night's catch of a rat, but with no luck so far. Other rats take the dead one in the night. So now we are going to use an egg. The trap is a square wire cage used to flop over a sitting goose to save it from foxes. The geese make nests in the long grass outside their pen which is flung right across the dam so they can swim in and out, as it is believed here that foxes can't swim. With the growth of the suburbs foxes are now coming into gardens and hunting close to houses. Last year Julie had to wrench a big white pet duck from a fox a few metres from the back door. It seemed incredible, yet I know it's true and the duck has never been the same again. Terrified and timid, it had a sort of nervous breakdown.

A spangled drongo is darting around chasing a white butterfly. Julie says this is a new bird here, so we looked it up. Black, sparkling, a red eye, it likes to sit in the open on posts or telegraph wires. Butcher birds are calling their sweet song. It may be the hour of the day, late afternoon, or that the mowing Julie's done has brought them out to look for worms.

Natali looked up from studying when I whistled to show her a grey cuckoo in the banana tree nearby. I walked over, interrupting her more to ask her to help me identify the bird.

Sam, turning the clock hands by standing on a chair, made it four o'clock, the hour he had been told we'd walk down to the river, after which Natali would play Monopoly with him. She is sitting here at the dining table explaining rules to him as he counts his moves out loud. The light is falling through her fair curls and on her face, shading her neck like a Caravaggio painting. She looks like the girl who modelled for Judith slaying Hollefernes. "I may be in gaol, but at least I'm rich," she says, gathering up her money.

Now to block the back entrance of the fowl pen so that tomorrow morning two roosters and a drake can be caught. The sun is setting, ripples are curving over the dam. The children are showering.

"Have you ever seen a rooster swim?" Julie called as we stood by the two young goats nuzzling us as we rolled out wire netting, measuring it to put around the carob tree they'd been eating. I looked and a black and white speckled-tailed rooster with its bright red comb was gliding earnestly across the dam to reach the side from which it had been cut off. "They don't swim for pleasure, but they can swim," she said, cutting the wire with clippers.

Last week Anton caught a dhufish. Its wings are in the freezer and given to me for fricassee tonight.

5th July, Friday. Elanora.

The olive green river is glinting in the late afternoon sun. Natali has just come into the bedroom where I lay reading, answering my question, "I'm doing my maths homework. It's so logical and boring, I'm going to start on Keats." She is now throwing bread at the geese in the orchard.

Sheridan flew home yesterday after making us two self-saucing chocolate puddings. One for dinner, because John arrived last night with his girls Donna and Stephanie, and the other for tonight. I roasted the drake but it took so long the children had to be fed with mashed potatoes and roast sweet potato and pieces from the bantam rooster in the Chinese broth from lunch. The bird was so wild it was dark, like pheasant.

Living here with Natali is like living with a laughing dolphin. Sam is so entranced by her he bought her oval lapis lazuli earrings. I helped him find them, thinking they were for his mother.

"Are you going to post them to her or wait till you get home?"

"I'm going to give them to her today. They're for Natali."

Flummoxed, thinking of the sum I'd put towards them, I asked, "Why are you giving them to Natali?"

"Because she bought me some lollies and she's been very nice to me."

Opening them, laughing with joy, Natali put them on with her astonished mother watching saying "Oh, they are so beautiful Sam! What wonderful taste you've got." She's worn them ever since except in the surf or the shower. Sam sat secretly under the dining room table writing a letter to Natali which he gave to her with a bunch of flowers from the garden. "Don't you think I'd better wake Natali, she won't know where we are," he said before leaving to go with John and his girls to Dreamland this morning.

I am amazed to see the effects of love on this boy. Reading a story by Paul Jennings to him about a boy in love with an ice statue in a shop window, turning pages faster, I hurried on, reading less and less until I whizzed past and found another story. I couldn't bear him to be more affected and influenced by romantic love, its madness and its glory. I wanted to protect him and keep him a child a little longer.

Natali said, "Oh Sam if only you were ten years older!"

Blue smoke against the light streams up behind the hill, veiling the trees on the higher one behind. Each afternoon this smoke begins. It is not sugar cane burning, because it's on a hill. I don't know what is burning. The poinsettia tree has its long brown pods falling on the drive. Behind me the huge bauhinia tree, taller than the house, lets down its carpet of pink blossom on the washing. An ibis standing as if turned to stone is on the lawn waiting for an insect.

Reading H. Kitto's *The Greeks*, one of Natali's books, I see Pelops is the Greek word for red-faced. I am pelops today as an allergy to grass has not abated. My hands look terrible. I do not look in the mirror. The skin, the largest organ in the body, is so vulnerable so I scratch. It's worse in the night. A vague irritability is the result and here it seems a waste amongst a ravishing landscape. Spiders' threads glint in the sun, linking thick plants to each other as we are linked by threads of something less visible and even stronger, call it love. And here are two magpies stalking round the corner like undertakers with a plan. Each morning they sing their song among the crows' beautiful ugly call.

"Oh! I stink of goat and horse!" says Natali walking up to this mango tree where I sit.

"I've been reading your Kitto" I say. "I hope you haven't been needing it."

"No, I got it from the Tugan secondhand bookshop. I'm not studying it. I'm just reading widely on the subject."

"There is a most beautiful beginning to this book, Natali. Listen.

'The reader is asked, for the moment, to accept this as a reasonable statement of fact, that in a part of the world that had for centuries been civilised, and quite highly civilised, there gradually emerged a people, not very numerous, not very powerful, who had a totally new conception of what human life was for, and showed for the first time what the human mind was for ... It would be ... true ... to say that while the older civilisations of the East were often extremely efficient in practical matters and, sometimes, in their art not inferior to the Greeks, yet they were intellectually barren. For centuries, millions of people had had experience of life – and what did they do with it? Nothing. The experience of each generation (except in certain purely practical matters) died with it – not like the leaves of the forest, for they at least enrich the soil. That which distils, preserves and then enlarges the experience of a people is Literature ..."'

And with that we parted, she knotting her hair onto the top of her head, going to shower.

6th July, Saturday. Elanora.

Oh, a windy day. The bauhinia tree is showering us in pink. Natali came out this morning saying, "I've found a good book of poetry. It's got everything: limericks, Yeats, Shelley, Byron, it's even got Keats."

7th July, Sunday. Elanora.

We have been to the monthly Byron Bay market. Youths under the mats of knotted hair strolled around with a naked child or two tagging along. They looked forlorn or somehow lost. But they must be happy with their green eyeshadow, their ragged clothes of drooping scarves, their beautiful bare brown arms, smooth and lovely. The smell of dope wafted around. People sold old clothes, bits of drainpipe, small whales made of pottery, bowls that looked as if the syrup spilt in them and got roasted in, homemade jewellery, vegetarian food, honey, jams, organic produce. Natali bought an empty book covered in pink fur. I could barely look at it.

A youth with long blonde hair, wearing only a top hat and a pair of trousers, swallowed a sword and, Sam says, bent over with it still inside. Rick, Julie and Anton's 19-year-old son, drove us.

At Hastings Bay he said, "There's a whale breaching!"

We stopped and went back. Four whales seemed to frolic. It looked like play the way they threw up plumes of water. Their tails glinted in the sun. People were standing on the headland watching, about forty or so. The whales were heading north, travelling in a line, a smaller one behind. We went on our way uplifted.

Byron Bay is a mecca for youth from all over the world. The blue glittering bay, backpackers' hostels. Inland the mountains and banana plantations, dope crops and huts in the hills. The public toilets were fairly new and painted prettily, yet inside the utmost squalor. This, I suppose, is the effect of drugs.

As we walked to the car I said, "Lord, I think they should put up a big university here, it's the only thing that I can think of that might help."

Natali asked why. I said it was because it makes me feel sad to see young people who look so lost. Perhaps that is just a projection of mine, but they are worshipping magic, cards, feathers, crystals, palm readers, everything, and yet there are perfectly good religions that have stood the test of time; with beautiful literature and a moral reasoning to them. Here they put their trust in the fall of a card or the gleam of a piece of glass. It's tragic.

Natali had read Keats in the car up the coast, curled up in the back asking "What is the difference between aeriel and ethereal?" She goes to a non-denominational school and does not, she tells me, believe in God. "I'd like to believe in reincarnation, but I can't."

"These people, Natali, seem like those Kitto writes of, who pass not even as leaves of the forest, with no art of anything but the most fatuous, vapid kind. I mean, it was one thing when it was genuine social revolution in the Seventies. There was the Peace movement over the Vietnam War which gave some political rigour to it, but now it seems so weak, so empty."

"Rebels without a cause" she said.

Rings in their noses like bulls and as easily led.

It seemed like a circus, or a gypsy camp. Something wild, strange and even threatening. So it may be that my feelings were so coloured by some threat, the horrific toilet, the smell of the drugs and a life of such ease and innocence that one might drown in its honey.

8th July, Monday. Elanora.

"Did you hear the rain in the night?" Natali asked coming from her bedroom. "It was like somebody whispering. So beautiful."

Natali and Sam are in the orchard now gathering golf balls.

I have just had a letter from Jack Morris, a Jesuit priest who works in the Sudan:

> You may marvel at the birth-rate here, and even have negative judgements about it. But imagine the grim surroundings, lack of beauty – no gardens, no paint, ragged, unmendable clothing, shortages of food, medicine, soap. Last week I saw a row of eight or ten women marching single file with heavy loads of wood on their heads, sweat pouring down their faces. I was told the source of the wood was at least 20 hours away on foot, two ten-hour days. They would get by on one meal, and finally sell the wood for the equivalent of $1 or less. Why? They have babies to feed. What would the refugee scene be without children?

There has been civil war in the Sudan for about twenty years. I met Jack at Paraa on the Nile in Uganda where he had a few days leave. He was showing his brother from the USA around. We stayed in round mud huts. The only sounds I heard that night were the munchings of hippopotamus that come out of the Nile to graze in the dark. That, and the tremendous thunder storm.

> Yes, many babies are sick, and many die, and it is sad, and it is heart-wrenching, but by god these people have warm, soft and inviting, non-judgmental, trusting and compassionate hearts. And, strange as it seems, we all find astonishing happiness and gentleness among the people. I've come to wonder whether we in the western world with all of our expensive control mechanisms haven't pressed the human enterprise into a series of small boxes. Sure, to have a baby, or any member of the family, die is difficult, but is it, in the full schemes of faith, Hindu, Jewish, Christian, Buddhism, tragic? Perhaps death, more than any other event in our human journey, has the power to put us in contact with our deepest self. Again, the mystery behind those words of Jesus about choosing weakness to overcome evil and the foolish and lowly to

confound the wise. That's what the refugee adventure has been for me – I am constantly confounded and perplexed.

I'm totally convinced that babies and the children they turn into, above all else, keep a people sane and centred, bold and resilient, and without them the caution and rigidity, the fear and the cynicism of old age would take over. Birth control is necessary, but it isn't a simple issue. We cannot ignore the world population explosion and its consequences, but something is drastically askew in our human reasoning when the central redemptive power of the individual child becomes a source of confusion, guilt, and even anger rather than joy and a doorway to the deepest meaning of human existence. Wordsworth had it right when he said, 'the child is father of the man'. We do not raise the babies, nor instruct them, nearly as much as they us. Without them we are lost.

When I asked Jack why he had come out of retirement in Michigan to work in the refugee camps, he said "I needed to find a way to empty myself. I needed to be empty." This phrase "to be empty" rose up again in a little book I am reading. Christ, Paul tells us, emptied himself (*ekenosen*) and took the form of a slave. This *kenosis*, emptying, is what Jack meant and what he knew would make him free. It will make me so too. If I can only manage it.

In his letter, Jack goes on to describe the birth of a Sudanese baby born in the back of his pickup. A photograph of himself holding Violet Agnes one hour old is enclosed.

> The heavens were filled with angels – I saw them, and they were singing 'Glory to God in the highest, and peace on earth to all who have enough goodwill to appreciate the mystery of a baby.'

Later

Natali, reading the newspaper she bought because, as she says, she's addicted to papers, shrieked and said, "Did you know in Turkey there is the death penalty for oral sex?" Mopping the floor I stood in front of her, swivelling my head to indicate Sam behind me. "Did you know," she said to John the first night he was here, "that rich women have more orgasms than others?" And, yesterday in the car, Rick handed her a page of foil-wrapped tablets picked up from the floor of the car. "Oh, Mum gave me these, they're Mersyndol for period pain!" she exclaimed. Next week she will be seventeen. At that age I could not have pronounced the word period to a man, let alone to one who was nineteen years old.

"Beauty has death and danger as its neighbour" Kitto says. Natali in the first flush of her beauty calls the light to her. It is the kind of loveliness that Helen had.

> So did the Trojan princess sit on the tower. And they saw Helen coming to the Tower, and said to each other softly, in winged words: 'Small blame to the Trojans and the well-armed Achaeans that they suffer so long, and so bitterly, for one like that, lovely as a goddess…'

Rick comes every day to pay tribute. I found Sam this morning, pulling up the sheets on her bed, attempting to make it for her while she was out. Everyone's inspired.

"Can you whistle, Sam?" Natali asked at the table.

He replied with a thin note.

"Your teeth have a gap like mine. Let me see." Lifting his lip, she peered in. "It's alright, they will close up. Mine won't now. See that piece of flesh between then, its called a diasteme. Mine had to be cut out because it kept my teeth apart and they won't grow together now, it's too late."

So they continued to whistle to each other through the gaps in their teeth.

"As a child I was in love with white violets and I have never cared for any plant since then with such all-consuming delight." This is how Dr Miriam Rothschild describes the start of her passion for wild gardens.

Born in 1908, her garden is at Aston Wold in Northamptonshire, England. She had led the movement towards wild gardens, and says drolly,

> A wild garden gets out of control; it presents difficulties and problems unknown in more conventional gardening, merely because we old gardeners lack the knowledge which others have

gained from years of experience of the horticulture of cultivated varieties of plants. We have to experiment.

This noble old woman has invented a meadow's seed mixture she calls 'The Farmers Nightmare'; cornflowers, corncockles, oats, barley, corn marigolds and field bindweed. Visitors, she says, look uneasily at the creeperclad courtyard and say, "Surely no one can live here." This is exactly the kind of garden I would like. But I lack the nerve. Following fashion I hack and slash.

Yet each time I come home on the train I am so happy to stare out the window at the verge of coreopsis, the Easter lilies, grasses, pink roses climbing up the banks, the purple native wisteria, broom, many things, all untended and beautiful. Miriam Rothschild's love for white violets shows that strange thing that keeps people capable of sudden shafts of pure happiness even during times of sadness. It is the white violet factor, that deep pleasure over so small but rare a thing that is such a gift, such a grace.

Later

Here is Rick who is on holidays from art school in Brisbane, at the table drawing with Sam. Natali is on the couch reading, her legs crossed at the ankles.

"See Sam," Rick says, "you can draw the verandah right around the house, even if you can't see it all from where you'd be sitting. You can be a bird. Or you can be a tree and see everything. See, this is the kite. And what's this, it's the shed and here's one of the goats. Now you draw a peacock eh? Draw its tail up, very big. Put in the eyes." And so on.

Sam holds the crayon and turns his head around following the drawing across the page.

How can I tell you how beautiful it is here? The river bending round, where each night at dusk the sunset turns the water pink and gold. Above the river the white ibis fly in flocks to nest in trees on the far bank, like knots of white ribbons on the branches, filling the trees. They do not spread among all the trees, they choose two or three, crowd in and leave the others bare.

The peacocks display in the sun beneath the mango, lavish, incredible and wanton. Two white peacocks stagger around like brides under the white load of their veils. In the mornings Sam and I lie in my bed after he has drawn the curtains and we watch the wind blow the Japanese fish kite hanging from the verandah, the dovecote where a crow waits, the giant fig which breathes in and out like an animal. Underneath it the tractor sits until Anton comes to mow the meadow.

To see the meadows so divinely lie
Beneath the quiet of the evening sky
is how every day here ends. The joy this boy brings me, the pleasure of this place.

Tomorrow Sam takes his first trip alone on a plane, flying home to his mother.